Copyright © 2019 Barb McMinimy

All rights reserved. No part of this book may be reproduced or transmitted in any form or by any means electronic or mechanical including photocopying, recording, or by any information storage and retrieval system without permission in writing from the publisher.

Aurora Books, an imprint of Eco-Justice Press, L.L.C.

Aurora Books
P.O. Box 5409 Eugene, OR 97405
www.ecojusticepress.com

Love, Vera
By Barb McMinimy & Vera Penkova

St. Basil Cathedral photo by Alexander Savin
Cover Design by David Diethelm | Eco-Justice Press

Library of Congress Control Number: 2019933042
ISBN 978-1-945432-30-9

Love, Vera

A Russian and American Friendship

by
Barb McMinimy & Vera Penkova

Aurora Books
Eugene, Oregon, USA

Dedicated to Bonnie Talley and Valya Zharinova,
who made our friendship possible.

ACKNOWLEDGMENTS

Vera and I are grateful for those who helped make this book possible, starting with my husband Mac, who suggested that we should write our story. He used his incredible memory to recall many details from the past 28 years and gave us his unwavering support and encouragement.

Thank you to the members of Barb's writing group. Conrad Roemer, Deb Rands, and Bev Garrett offered Barb helpful suggestions at our weekly meetings during the past two years. Bonnie Olin taught Barb how to use applications for creating a digital manuscript and making the graph which is included as an addendum. Marc Laakso edited the final manuscript for errors. Ken Fenter spent untold hours preparing the final design — making digital copies of photos for the book and preparing the manuscript for uploading for printing.

Yadira Despaigne patiently tutored Barb in the computer skills needed to scan, edit and insert photos and make changes to the text.

Andrey (Andy) Penkov, Vera's son, scanned and emailed the newspaper articles and many of the photos that are a part of this book.

Nancy McDaniel read each new segment of our writing — asking questions, advising, and encouraging us during the past two years.

Emma Kim read the completed manuscript and made valuable suggestions, including introducing Barb to our publisher, David Diethelm.

Donna Skinner previewed our manuscript and wrote the Forward to our book. Her suggestions, praise and encouragement are truly appreciated by both authors.

Table of Contents

Letter From Moscow: Dear Mr. Mayor 1
A Warm Welcome 7
Getting Acquainted 13
Comparing Cultures 25
Hesston, Kansas 35
A Farewell With Little Hope 37
Difficult Times: A Crumbling Soviet Union 39
First Impressions — 1992 47
Night Train To St. Petersburg 59
Tourists In Moscow 65
Politicians From Pushkino 77
Hand-Carried Letters 79
Return To Russia — 1995 85
Letters And Phone Calls 97
Andy Takes A Risk 103
Enduring Friendship 105
About the Authors 109
Addenda 111

Forward

This heartwarming story of a decades long international friendship began around a kitchen table in Moscow in 1989. As the Soviet Union was breaking up, five Russian friends got the improbable idea of visiting the United States to learn first hand about the West. They had little money and lacked passports, visas, invitations, connections and a sense of U.S. culture or geography, but that did not curb their curiosity or enthusiasm. They wanted to travel for six months.

The five women drafted a letter expressing their interest in the trip for themselves along with three of their teenage children to see the U.S. They found a guide to colleges and universities in several states and wrote a generic letter addressed to "Dear Mr/Mrs Mayor" telling of their wish to travel. Then they sat down to hand write about 100 letters and randomly selected towns to receive the letters.

Maybe it was naive and audacious but it worked for them. Several towns responded with invitations. The small agricultural town of Garden City, Kansas, with an amazingly rich history of hosting foreign visitors, was among the first to respond. An energetic mayor and a local Sister Cities group took on the challenge to make the trip happen. This memorable human connection changed the lives of all of the visitors and all of the host families as well as the culture of Garden City.

Their book tells the story from the point of view of one of the Russian visitors (Vera Penkova) and her host family (Barbara and Milton McMinimy). It recounts the adventure and growing understanding that followed. They all saved letters, snapped photographs and took notes on their several visits across cultures, and their friendship continues almost 30 years later.

Characters

Americans

Barb and Milton (Mac) McMinimy — hosts for Vera
Bonnie Talley, Garden City's mayor — host for Valya and Masha
Donna and Gene Skinner — hosts for Tamara and Alex
Emily and Ted Barkley — hosts for Ira and Tim
Lina and Lee Schneller — hosts for Valentina
Zina Amante — Garden City resident from Belarus who translated for our guests
LeAnn and Stan Clark — Hesston, Kansas, hosts for Vera
Nancy and Sam Douglas — Kansas farmers who Vera and Andy visited in 1999

Russians who visited Garden City, Kansas

Vera Penkova and her son **Andrey Penkov (Andy)**
Tamara Soboleva and her son **Alex**
Ira (Irina) Tkacheva and her son **Tim**
Valentina Chirka
Valya (Valentina) Zharinova and her daughter **Masha**
Nikolay Klimchuk — mayor of Pushkino
Yuri Stepchinko — vice mayor of Pushkino
Little Yuri — choir member and artist from Pushkino

Russians Barb and Mac met during their visits in 1992 and 1995

Natasha and Alexander — St. Petersburg hosts for Barb and Mac
Victor Zharinov — Valya's husband
Sasha — Vera's brother
Vera's mother and father
Mary — the lady Vera bought her eggs from

Letter From Moscow: Dear Mr. Mayor

In late fall of 1989 my friend Valya approached me with a wild request. She asked me to translate a letter. It began like this: "Dear Mr/Mrs Mayor, We are five Russian women from Moscow very curious to see America and learn firsthand about its life and people." As I've said, it was 1989. Russia was living through the so-called "perestroika" (reconstruction). After decades of limitations we were allowed to travel to capitalist countries and see how life was there. Before that we could only judge about life in the rest of the world from official newspapers and magazines and TV programs, but it was always the same; average people suffered from bad capitalists. So my friend decided to jump at the chance and go and see for herself. She came across some American directories, where she found zip codes of some cities. (It was a directory of universities and colleges.) I translated the letter, laughing to myself at her crazy enterprise. I even helped to write the letters – there were about 100 of them – and forgot all about it. Early in 1990 letters started to arrive, inviting us to come! Only then did I realize that I had to make a decision. I hadn't given any thought to it before, as I was 100% sure our letters would be ignored.

After some thinking (not long, I must confess) I decided to go in for this adventure.

Now we had a choice to make. I don't remember the names of the cities that were writing to invite us – they were from different parts of the USA. We wrote back with more details, and very soon we got a letter from Garden City, Kansas. It was very enthusiastic and had some suggestions of how to arrange the trip. We thought, "These people definitely want to see us at their place and are ready to take actions." What is more, the name Garden City sounded great, especially in Russian winter. So we wrote a letter saying that we were writing to come and would need a formal invitation. That was done through the Sister Cities organization. They learned that Gary Price, Superintendent of schools for Hesston, Kansas, was going to Moscow early in the summer and

Love, Vera

asked him to meet with us and discuss the details.

Mr. Price, a very nice person, came to Moscow and brought the invitations and personal letters from the families who were going to be our hosts. He gave us each an ID badge in the shape of a sunflower, so that people who would be meeting us at the airport could recognize us. I got a short letter and a photo from a couple by the name of McMinimy. The man looked happy and perfectly relaxed, while his wife looked as if she realized what kind of adventure they'd gotten themselves into.

Barb and Milton (Mac) in February of 1990.

The letter was pretty short and formal. I remember one strange remark from it: "My husband can make bread." Did it mean that they assured me that bread, at least, I would have at their house? You should know the situation in Russia at that time. We hadn't been spoilt for choice before, but in those years there was lack of practically everything and we had to stand in long lines for simple food like cereals, butter, cheese, or meat.

In February of 1990 I was researching deeds at the courthouse in Goodland, Kansas, a two-hour drive from our home in Garden City, and a blizzard was approaching southwestern Kansas. That's when the phone call came that would change my life. "It's your husband," said the Register of Deeds. I anxiously picked up the extension and heard Mac say, "Mayor Bonnie Talley needs to know if we'll host a Russian woman for a few months, and she has to know right away."

"Let's talk about it when I get home," was my reply.

"She says it can't wait. She's meeting with the city council and has to have an answer immediately. Yes or No?" came his response.

In my rush to finish gathering data for my appraisal assignments and leave for home ahead of the rapidly approaching blizzard, I really couldn't focus on his question; so, after a slight hesitation, I said, "O.K."

Hosting people from other countries was not new to Mac and me. In July of 1976 we hosted a delightful young German couple who stayed with us in Kansas City for ten days during our country's bicentennial celebration, and they invited us to visit them a few years later. Mac and I had welcomed numerous Costa Ricans to our Garden City home during the 1980s and had enjoyed visiting our sister city, Ciudad Quesada, Costa Rica. But we knew nothing about the USSR, and now we were about to host a stranger from a Communist country.

Why would anyone want to visit our remote, industrial farming town on the high plains near the borders of Colorado and Oklahoma? We had left my friends and family and the restaurants and culture of Kansas City ten years earlier when Mac's job had brought us 350 miles away to Garden City, and adjusting to my new life in this rural town had not been easy for me.

Garden City (population 25,000) had two beef-packing plants and several feedlots; and the smell from the feedlots filled the air year-round. Local radio stations played country and western music, ranchers and cowboys were prevalent in the cafes and banks, and cattle auctions were advertised in the windows of businesses on Main Street. The annual Beef Empire Days celebration, with its parade, rodeo, and free barbecue feed was the major "cultural" event of the year. Many years of irrigating the surrounding fields of alfalfa, corn, soybeans, and wheat had caused the Arkansas River south of town to run dry; so, instead of providing water for boating or fishing, the river bed was a favorite place for young people with motorcycles. Mac and I would drive four hours to Colorado Springs or five hours to Denver several weekends a year for good restaurants and fresh air. So, we wondered why five ladies from Moscow would want to visit our town.

Like many Americans, I had heard of Perestroika and Glasnost in the late 1980s under Mikhail Gorbachev; but I really had no idea how that was affecting Russian citizens. Land was restored to the citizens, and cooperatives and privately owned businesses were now legal. Political prisoners were released, freedom of speech was permitted, and banned literature could now be published. As news from CNN became available to ordinary citizens in Moscow, uncensored live TV coverage of the Soviet legislative deliberations allowed people to witness the Communist leadership being questioned and held accountable. In the summer of 1989, an estimated two million people joined hands to form a human chain 370 miles across Estonia, Latvia,

Love, Vera

and Lithuania; and newscasters announced the withdrawal from the Soviet Union by the satellite states.

The fall of the Berlin Wall on November 29th, 1989, brought the beginning of the reunification of Germany and was followed in December of 1989 by Gorbachev and George H. W. Bush's announcement of the end of the Cold War. When Vera and her friends realized that Russian citizens could travel out of the country and return home free from interrogation by authorities, they started making plans to come to the United States.

The Sister Cities Committee met for breakfast for an "emergency" board meeting a day or two after Bonnie received the letter that had been mailed from Moscow to "Mr/Mrs Mayor, Garden City, Kansas, USA". Five women and their three teenagers wanted to visit the U.S. for six months and were asking for an invitation so they could apply for their visas. Bonnie answered our skeptical questions: "Is this a scam? Do they want money?" She passed their letter around the table, saying that the ladies only wanted to experience living in America. "I'm sure it's not a scam; they only need an official invitation," she assured us. "They're not asking for money." So, we voted unanimously to have Bonnie invite the ladies, providing the committee members would not be responsible for financing their trip.

The preparation for our trip started. Work began in three directions. One was to get the American visas. We also had to buy plane tickets, which wasn't easy, as there were just a few flights to America at that time. And one more thing—we needed American dollars, and we could exchange our rubles only in one place in Russia — all banks belonged to the government, and there was one bank in Moscow where we could exchange money, providing we had an official permit. Such a task meant standing in lines, and it wasn't a few-hour-affair or even a few-day one; we registered in the "lines" and for about four months came once a week or so to confirm that we were still willing to reach its end!

Then quite an unexpected thing happened. I had been planning to get married before the whole adventure started and then, right in the middle of our preparation, I realized I was pregnant! My first thought was to bow out — how can I go exploring a new world? But it was my Mum who reassured me.

She had given birth to three children and stayed active until the very day. My boyfriend Sergi added that I might be even safer in the U.S., considering the situation in Russia at the time. To tell the truth, I was at first disappointed with my family — they gave their consent so quickly! On the other hand, I had put in so much effort already and had great expectations; and the other women urged me to go, because they spoke very little English and relied on me. They promised to spare me in every possible way if I went. Soon the decision was made in favour of the trip.

❊

As constitutional reform in Russia was underway (the Russian Soviet Federative Socialist Republic (RSFSR) was formed in June of 1990), letters were flowing between Garden City and Moscow to get a formal invitation and visas for our five visiting Russian ladies and their three children. In the last week of November of 1990 they were beginning their adventure in America.

The Russian government would allow the travelers to bring only $300 each on their trip. They planned to all live together, with the women working to pay for food and rent while the three teenagers attended school. We knew their plan to find jobs was unrealistic and that they would not be able to afford to live in the U.S. without more money. So Bonnie went into high gear, speaking to numerous service organizations, churches, committees, etc., in Garden City and surrounding communities and "passing the hat" to raise funds for her cause. She then arranged the purchase of eight train tickets from Washington, D.C., to Garden City and contacted her sources in D.C. to meet our visitors at the airport, take them to meet with Nancy Kassebaum (the junior senator from Kansas), provide overnight lodging, and then transport them to the train station on the following day.

Love, Vera

A Warm Welcome

The departure day – Nov. 27, 1990, came. We had everything – the visas, the tickets and 300 dollars each! What we lacked was the understanding of what was ahead. Little did we know about life in America, and I felt like an astronaut going to Mars. Being a student of English at University, I had read quite a lot of books by American authors such as Theodore Dreiser, Steinbeck, Vonnegut, and Hemingway. I had seen a few American films too. (When I started to talk with my new American friends about American writers, they were quite surprised at the choice – we seemed to have been reading different literatures. They are well-read people, and they had their own list of authors! I've been trying to catch up with them ever since.) Before "perestroika", the official propaganda depicted America as an evil state plotting against the whole world. Later, at the end of 1980, they started to refer to the U.S. and Western Europe as "civilized countries", whatever that meant – we were to find out.

On the morning of Nov. 27 we arrived in Washington – five women and three children. We recognized the people meeting us by sunflowers they were holding. They were from the Sister Cities organization. They took us to the hotel. I was amazed at how smooth the road was – in Russia roads were quite bumpy at the time. The car was very comfortable, unlike cars in Russia. At the hotel – the rooms looked grand – we were given the itinerary. The other women were curious about what was in it, but I told them it didn't seem to be ours, as "there was something about meeting a Senator". It was past bedtime in Russia and we were exhausted, so we went to bed and hardly had fallen asleep when there was a loud knock on the door and an urgent voice asked, "Are you ready to go to the Senate? Senator Kassabaum is expecting you." What? The Capitol? The Senator? The women asked me if that was in the itinerary, and it was, but I hadn't taken it seriously!

We were going to speak to an American Senator on the very first day in the U.S.! We were five Russian women from different walks of life, but none of us had anything to do with politicians. It was only possible at that time when the

Love, Vera

Iron Curtain had fallen down and we on both sides longed to learn about each other. I think we felt we had been deprived of the possibility of friendship between our two great nations and were eager to catch up on it. I was so overwhelmed at the immensity of the event that I hardly remembered what we had talked about. I'm sure it was politics — we were not very happy about our president Gorbachev, and I think we discussed that and also spoke about the changes happening in Russia at the time.

Senator Nancy Kassebaum and staff members in Washington, D.C. with our Russian visitors.

I remember vaguely that we had a short tour of the Capitol and then went to some Washington museums — I was exhausted and excited at the same time and very thankful for the warm welcome we got from those unknown friends from Sister Cities. (We didn't know at the time what a really warm welcome was — wait till we arrive in Garden City the next day.) We departed on a train to Chicago, where we changed for the train to Garden City. All the people we met were friendly and helpful, and we were beginning to feel more and more at ease.

Having traveled ten hours on the plane, I was too tired to notice many things. I couldn't help comparing America with Russia, labeling everything "better or worse". First, the highway was so smooth that we could easily have a cup of coffee, which would be impossible in Russia with its bumpy roads. Also, we didn't have air conditioning in cars and would drive with the windows down, and the exhaust fumes spoiled the pleasure of traveling. American cars, of course, were much more comfortable.

However, there were some things that I rated as "worse". When we were touring Washington, I noticed that our guide had to pay for parking. That was unheard of in Russia at the time. There were so few cars that you could park practically anywhere without having to pay. Also, when we were buying some snacks in a shop, we were surprised at how thin the slices of ham and bread were! And we didn't like the bread at all. I then remembered Barb's phrase, "My husband can make bread". Bread is not tasty in Russia now, too, and I had to learn how to make bread myself.

Still, another thing, when we boarded the overnight train from Chicago to Garden City, we were surprised when we didn't find compartments for sleeping – there were just train cars with chairs like on the bus. In Russia traveling by train was much more comfortable, with full size beds so that you could sleep comfortably during the night. We had some sleep of course – we were awfully tired. Besides, we were so overwhelmed with all those new experiences that little did we worry about what was ahead of us.

We had all the reasons for worrying, though, having to stay with people we didn't know at all for as long as six months, depending on them for everything. Even now I feel bewildered about what could have happened if our relationship had gone wrong! Anyway, by the end of the journey we were totally exhausted and ready for anything.

Fred Brooks, was the editor of the newspaper and published many editorials and articles over the next several months, stirring up interest about the visitors from Moscow. Other committee members began arranging for the ladies to give talks about life in Russia to various groups in the area, suggesting they receive a small "speaker's fee" each time they gave a program. Someone purchased small American and Soviet flags, and Donna Skinner, one of the hosts, made a large Soviet flag for the front door of each host family.

On the morning of November 29th, 1990 (one year after the Berlin Wall came down), about 80 people gathered at the train station to welcome our Russian guests, filling the little depot with balloons, flowers, and American and Soviet flags. I was quite amused when I noticed two handsome young cowboys sitting in front of a large red Soviet flag, seemingly

Waiting inside the Garden City train depot.

Love, Vera

bewildered by the surrounding commotion.

The Amtrak agent stepped up on a bench and made a dramatic show of loudly announcing the train's approach before leading everyone outside to the platform. As the visitors stepped off the train, they were surrounded by TV cameras, radio and news reporters, city and county commissioners, dozens of interested townspeople, five host families, and Zina Amante, a local Russian who would interpret. (Vera told me later that she kept looking around for those important dignitaries who the people must be waiting for, not realizing it was her group that we were greeting.) After everyone gathered inside the depot, Bonnie introduced our guests to the crowd. Tamara Soboleva (a physics teacher) and her son, Alex, Irina Tkacheva (a computer programmer) and her son, Tim, and Valentina Chirka (a medical biologist) were welcomed by their host families. Valentina (Valya) Zharinova (a programmer) and her daughter, Masha, would be staying with Bonnie, and Vera (an English teacher) would be with Mac and me. Zina planned to translate for us, but Vera handled the interviews beautifully; and I sighed with relief that we would have no trouble communicating with our house guest.

Russian visitors arriving at the Garden City train depot on November 29, 1990.

Mac and I drove Vera down Garden City's Main Street on the way home and then past the old two-story homes near downtown, the library, our church, and along several blocks of residences before pulling into our driveway, the house with a Soviet flag hanging on the front door to welcome her. I thought she was just being camera-shy when she tried to avoid having her photo taken with the balloon and flag and learned later that she was only nervous about the Soviet flag. She told me several weeks later, "I had traveled so far to get away from Communism and thought I was going to be staying with a Communist host family!" Her father was a member of the Communist party until he retired, but only to keep his job; and her grandmother had taken Vera "secretly" to the Russian Orthodox Church to be baptized. (Her Father supposedly didn't know this until after he retired.)

We arrived in Garden City in the morning of the next day, and the minute we stepped off the train we found ourselves in the middle of some mystery. Of course we had expected a warm welcome from the people who had already done so much for us to be able to come. But the welcome we got exceeded all our wildest expectations. The platform was crowded with people, all smiling broadly and looking as if they were meeting their closest relatives. We would have thought it had nothing to do with us (like with the itinerary in Washington, D.C.) had they not been holding Soviet flags! "Communists," I thought." They are all communists, the whole city of them! That's why they have invited us." What a terrible disappointment! We hoped we had escaped from the Soviet regime. All in vain. I remember thinking, "Stupid! You were hoping to escape, but communists are everywhere; it's total. Now you will have to spend another few months among them, and it seems they look even more enthusiastic than in Russia." To crown it all, they were playing the Soviet anthem! It all went in my mind very quickly.

Meanwhile, people started to speak to us. There were reporters from the local radio, TV and newspaper. They asked questions. Since I was to do most of the talking, I tried my best to say something – I was so overwhelmed with emotions that I am sure all I said was very stupid. (I could have said any nonsense.) Strangely, I don't remember clearly first meeting all those people, even Barb and Milton McMinimy, who would become my friends for life. After a while I found myself in their car going 'home'. I don't remember what we talked about and if we talked at all. It wasn't easy to start a conversation, I guess, especially being complete strangers. What I remember clearly is my surprise when on our approach the garage door opened by itself! I hadn't heard anything about remote control, and I thought I was in a fairy tale and it was a miracle, like Ali Baba's "Open Sesame". Another surprise was when we stepped into the house right from the garage. In Russia even if you were

Love, Vera

lucky enough to have a car and even luckier to have a garage, you had to walk home, and quite often it would be a few-minutes walk!

There was still another surprise inside the house! There was a big red flag on the door! When I saw it, my hope that at least my host family was not Communist vanished. There I was in the middle of America, doomed to live among over-enthusiastic Communists! When later I spoke to my new American friends, I shared my fears with them. They laughed and said they had hoped the red flag would help me feel at home. In fact, all the host families had Soviet flags — and it had taken them quite an effort! When I think of that, I love them even more.

Getting Acquainted

After showing Vera around our house and putting her things into the guest bed-room, I invited her to go with me to the grocery store to buy dog food.

"You have special food for dogs?" she asked me.

"You don't?" was my reply. It was only the first step toward our learning about each other's culture. I had no idea what it was like to shop for food in Russia, but I could tell from the amazed look on Vera's face as we walked slowly up and down the aisles that what she saw was a little overwhelming. By the time we paused at the end of the long aisle containing nothing but pet food, I was becoming embarrassed at the abundance of Americans and was beginning to realize the large gulf between our two countries. A year and a half later we visited her home, and I could finally understand why she was so surprised. (But that's another chapter of this story.)

Bonnie and the members of the Sister Cities Committee had arranged a very full speaking schedule for our eight Russian guests, so they had very little time to rest after their exhausting travels through nine time zones. Residents of Garden City welcomed them at a pot luck held at the Community Congregational Church the evening after their arrival, and each rather nervous guest was introduced. I can't imagine how tired they must have been, but they were gracious guests and posed in front of the Christmas tree before going to their homes for some rest.

We wanted our guests to experience the daily life of ordinary Americans, including shopping. After seeing Vera's reaction to her first experience at the grocery store, I was somewhat puzzled when she didn't comment during our visit to the women's shops and the nicest

Love, Vera

FRONT: Valentina, Alex, Masha, Valya, Tim BACK: Vera, Tamara, Ira.

jewelry store on Main Street. I would learn later that what appeared to the American consumer as an elegant display of products, with open spaces highlighting only a few items placed on shelves, was perceived by my Russian friend as scarcity. Similarly, that special Christmas dinner prepared for our guests at the country club and presented so elegantly by the proud chef had been seen by the Russians as a sparse meal on a very large plate!

When Vera and Valya discovered Walmart, with its abundance and low prices, they thought they had found a gold mine! They could walk a mile from our house, purchase a few items, and walk back home in just a couple of hours, rather than spending their entire day standing in long lines for a few poor quality goods. I never understood their excitement until Mac and I visited Vera in the summer of 1992 and saw the nearly empty shelves in their State shops.

Most of the host families had busy lives, so we coordinated with each other to drive our guests to tours of the city hall, county courthouse, hospital, newspaper, etc. As a real estate appraiser with my own business, I was able to arrange my schedule so I could attend several of these tours, and my favorite was one of the local banks where we were shown the vault with gold bars. I was sorry to miss the tour of the fish farm (yes, in Kansas), and I made sure to be "too busy" on the day they toured the Iowa Beef packing plant a few miles outside of town.

An excited Valentina holding a one-thousand-dollar bill.

The next few days were hell. The whole town had been looking forward to meeting the Russians for so long. And people wanted to be the first to meet us. Imagine being introduced to crowds of people all day long. I honestly tried to memorize who was who. But all I could remember was smiling faces and names that wouldn't stick right. I guess there were many awkward moments. Thank God people just smiled and generously forgave my mistakes. By the way, while still in Russia we had heard a lot about "plastic" smiles so typical of Americans. The general belief was that a person can't smile all the time. I had been told: "Don't trust them when they smile at you; that could only mean they want to hide their true feelings." Well, there I was surrounded by smiling people and I had no reason to get suspicious of their feelings. I even smiled back, rarely though it might have seemed to my new American friends — I'm not the one to waste my smiles! By and by, I got used to sleeping when it was daytime in Russia and being surrounded by crowds of people asking questions. I found myself enjoying the company of my new friends more and more.

When we were leaving Moscow we were allowed to take three hundred dollars each. It cost us a lot of rubles and time because we had to register in the bank and regularly go there to confirm that we still wanted to exchange our money. (To think I had spent all my savings on the exchange and the ticket

Love, Vera

and even worried about it; and then the new government robbed us, devaluing our savings overnight in 1991!) We realized that those three hundred dollars wouldn't be enough to last us for six months, and we had asked about any possibilities to find jobs. But the organizers said we wouldn't be able to get any legal jobs. What we didn't know was that we would be engaged in every possible activity in Garden City; and believe me it was a full-time job and often long hours, because Garden Citizens like to live life to the full.

The mayor of the city, Bonnie Talley, had written in the local newspaper before we arrived: "They will be scheduled to speak at most of the service clubs in the three months they will be here. If you have any events you want to share with them, please call..." I am perfectly sure there was no event in the city and any other place around it that went without us. Or at least one of us — we often had to split because there were two or more social functions we were scheduled to visit at the same time. Quite often my day began with an appointment for breakfast with some women — thank God men were busy at work — then a meeting at a women's group or church and then dinner at some club. Of course, I was tired of that intense socializing program, but I'm sure that in the long run we all got to know each other's cultures and ways better.

Bonnie introducing Tamara at the Sister Cities banquet.

The ladies had brought slides to share with their new American friends, and they soon found themselves speaking at numerous churches, service group lunch meetings, etc. At first, Vera, with her excellent English, was the spokesperson for the group; but by January, one or two of the ladies began speaking to groups while Vera was scheduled at a different meeting. Zina, our local Garden City resident from Belarus, attended those meetings to translate.

Bonnie was present at most of the meetings; and the children, ages 13 and 14, often attended with their moms to help with translating or answering questions from the audience.

Ira presenting a program, with help from her son Tim.

We had been kept busy for two months with a short break for Christmas. I loved American Christmas! The houses were beautifully decorated. It got dark early, and I enjoyed our drives in town and looking at the houses. The shops got busier, and there was Christmas music everywhere. That was the first time I heard Christmas songs and loved them so much that Barb gave me a cassette to take home. Barb and Milton took me on a wonderful trip to Colorado for Christmas. (Thank you, dear friends.)

Several host families took their visitors to Colorado during the Christmas holiday season for downhill skiing. Vera loved to cross-country ski in Russia but would not be skiing until after her baby was born; so Mac drove the three of us to Colorado Springs, about a four-hour drive away, for a relaxing weekend. The month of December seemed to have flown by so quickly. Vera had been scheduled for meetings and tours nearly every day since her arrival, and this trip was the first time we could relax and talk about her impressions of our country and the many political changes happening in the Soviet Union. I loved that Christmas trip to Colorado, and I have always been grateful that Vera's strong English and broad interests allowed us to talk about a wide variety of topics, including our views on politics and religion.

Love, Vera

By New Year's Eve, everyone had returned from their holiday trips, and they gathered at our house for a traditional Russian New Year's Eve meal. While the ladies prepared the food in the kitchen, the children played with our dog in the basement recreation room and the adults visited or danced to the Russian music our guests had brought with them. The evening's highlight was the midnight presentation of a traditional Russian cake, and champagne toasts, of course.

Valya instructing Masha while Ira and Vera chop vegetables.

Mac dancing with Valentina and Tamara in our living room.

After we returned to Garden City, the talks started again. By that time we had met practically everybody who ever wanted to see us, and the generous people of GC decided to share us with the nearby towns. We visited Ashland, Kismet, Lakin, Liberal, Plains, etc. Everywhere we went we met friendly people who were genuinely interested in our country.

I especially remember meeting with the city clergymen. When I was told I was going to give a talk to them, I did my best to turn that offer down. Who was I to enlighten pastors about Russian culture and religion? But you should know Bonnie Talley — there was no escape from her grip. I knew it very well by that time. The best I could do was to concentrate and recall everything I'd ever learned from books or heard from people. I even went to the library to look up some dates from history.

Religion was not officially banned in the USSR (That would be too much even for the Communists.), but there was an active propaganda against it. While at school and later at university, I was taught to be an atheist, and we were made aware that we might get in trouble should we start going to church. My Grandma believed in God. (She was born in 1905 and grew up in a religious family.) However, she started to go to church when she was quite old. There were very few churches. For example, in my home town with the population of nearly a million there were two churches. And those were closely supervised by the local authorities and, as a result, were empty most of the time. I'm very thankful to my Grandma who had courage to bring me to church to baptize me when I was a baby. And she was my Godmother, since there was nobody else! It might be because of that I'd been interested in religious matters and tried to find any information on religion. So I did have some knowledge, but it was definitely not enough for the clergymen.

I was awfully nervous at the beginning of my talk, thinking, "Please, God, don't let them ask tricky questions". Thank God, the audience was most understanding; they made me at ease from the start. They did ask a lot of questions and showed special interest in the personal part of my talk. I even got applause at the end ... and an invitation to give another talk! I had to own up that I'd run out of information on that subject. We laughed (They thought it to be a joke and I knew it was true.), and we said good-bye.

We went on giving talks without days off, traveling to distant towns and sometimes staying overnight. By 15th January, my birthday, I was very tired of spending so much time in public. Barb asked how I would like to spend that day. I answered, "I want to stay at home. The whole day. Alone." I was generously granted that opportunity, although I guess people were surprised – especially since we were going to Moscow, Kansas, that day. But I really needed that day away from everybody – I'm not an outgoing person and was used to having my private space. Barb and Milton gave me a cassette recorder for my birthday – a very useful thing for a teacher of English.

Mac and I continued showing Vera as many aspects of American life as we could think of. He drove her to his family's ranch two hours from Garden City to meet his mother. I introduced her to my friends. She and I went to a meeting of my book group. One day we even visited a mortuary owned by a friend of mine; she seemed surprised

Love, Vera

at the luxury and variety of the caskets. Another time I took her with me to help measure a house I was appraising and tried to explain to her why banks needed an appraisal. When she asked why Mac and I worked so many hours every week, I showed our utility bills and mortgage payments to her. Then I explained about real estate taxes and payments for our house, car, and health insurance. I laughed when she looked amazed and said, "You buy health insurance so you never get sick?"

❋

Originally we came to explore America and get new experiences, and people we met in Garden City were as eager to learn about life in the Soviet Union as we wanted to get to know about theirs. It was a new experience for both sides, and we spent hours that grew into days, weeks and months talking. There were so many enjoyable meetings which enriched our lives. And it became possible, thanks to the enthusiasm of many people in Garden City.

Bonnie Talley, the mayor of GC, was the heart and soul of all the events. She was a warm, ever-smiling, enthusiastic and awfully energetic person. She generated ideas, rushed into any activity and infected everybody with her enthusiasm. She was a retired teacher, and of course, as any teacher, she knew exactly what people were to do; she gave orders and kept everybody busy. As a politician, she knew how to make you feel special and you immediately agreed to do what she suggested. She was in her late sixties and not what you would call slim, and she rushed in her car from one function to another and seemed to be everywhere, smiling her warm reassuring smile.

Once she took us on a wonderful trip to Topeka. She went there on business — there was a meeting of mayors. It was a long trip, and she sped all the way. We had some free time while Bonnie was at the meeting, so we went for a walk. We didn't go very far when we found ourselves in a very poor district. It was quite surprising, as in GC we had never seen poor dwellings. We had thought that everyone in America was rich or very rich. In the evening we were invited to dinner in the Capitol, where we talked about Russia and our impressions of America. We got a very warm welcome and enjoyed a wonderful dinner. The dinner was held on the top level of the Capitol, and we enjoyed the spectacular view of the night streets decorated for Christmas. It was there that I tasted that divine soup, clam chowder. That's the dish I would prefer to any other. It's a pity we don't have such soup in Russia.

Donna and Gene Skinner hosted Tamara and her son, Alex. Donna contributed a lot to the whole adventure. She's a very well-educated person, amazingly curious about life, very kind and always ready to help. She taught at the community college at the time (Of course, we gave a talk there.), and she participated in many activities. I loved talking to her – she is so knowledgeable and has a wonderful sense of humor. By the way, it was her idea to make the red flags.

TWO SPECIAL LADIES: Donna on the left — Bonnie on the right.

Emily and Ted Barkley hosted Irina and her son, Tim. Ted worked for the city administration, and it was he who arranged our weekly telephone chats with our families in Russia. Although Emily was a mother of two little boys and pregnant, she and her husband were involved in every activity in the city. I couldn't understand how Emily managed. It was she who helped me to realize that you can have little children and yet be socially active.

Now about my nearest and dearest – my host family. Whenever I think of them, and it is very often, I have this tide of warm feelings in my heart, like when you think about family. I truly believe it was a miracle meeting Barb and Milton. Imagine, we wrote more than 90 letters to different places in America and chose GC at random, just because they were the first to send the invitations, traveled thousands of miles from one social system into another, and found friends for life!

It wasn't love at first sight, though. I remember that our first days together were pretty awkward; we were complete strangers and needed some time to find topics for conversations. For me, everything was new and different and I felt terribly shy at first. The house seemed luxurious to me. In Russia I lived with my Granny in a three-roomed apartment and shared the bathroom and the kitchen with the neighbor. In McMinimy's house I had a bedroom and a bathroom for myself. Of course, my friends did everything possible to make me feel at home, and I felt their reassurance all the time. Barb would often say they were lucky to have me at their house, but I realized that although the house was big for its owners to share their living space, I was depriving them of the privacy they were used to. I felt guilty.

Barb and Milton both worked, and for Milton, a CPA, it was his busiest season at work. He didn't have any days off. Nevertheless, he spared his time to go to different functions or take me to places. Barb also had to combine work and taking care of me. I'm very grateful to them both, for without them I would have been completely helpless — I didn't have the money, I didn't know the city and wouldn't have been able to get around. I guess for them, it was like adopting a child except children are much more fun. And they did have to teach me many things. For example, I couldn't operate some things in the kitchen, like the microwave or the coffee machine. The most difficult was the tin-opener, though. Whenever I tried to manage it, the tin would drop with whatever was in it all over the place. It was easier with the coffee machine — I didn't drink coffee at all. I was surprised to find out that Americans drank so much coffee and ignored tea. Barb remembered that her mother had once given her a teapot, and we started to drink tea together. She spoiled me, buying very good tea in special shops, the kind of tea I had never had before — I still remember its taste. It seemed funny to them that I drank hot tea, and I hadn't heard of iced tea before. When I ordered tea at a restaurant, they would bring me iced tea, so I had to explain that I wanted hot tea. Then I got lukewarm tea. As it happened again and again, I decided to stop asking for tea at all and drank something else. I hope I wasn't very naughty otherwise and ate and drank all American food, and as a rule I liked it.

I guess by and by I was becoming more adjusted to the new way of life, and it would have been easier for Barb had it not been for the greatest surprise — my being pregnant. I thought it was my own concern and didn't tell Barb at once; I mentioned this fact only after a while. When Barb heard about it, she was shocked; it was evident. Being a terribly responsible person, Barb took it as if she had to monitor the situation — and she did. She immediately arranged for me to see the doctor. It was Doctor Welch, and although I felt wonderful and didn't need to see a doctor, she made some checks. I visited her a few times during my stay, and she didn't charge any money. (Thank you, Doctor Welch! I hope you are enjoying life and your children make you happy. Thank you, Barb.)

Later Barb started going to the hospital with me, where they taught pregnant women. Spending so much time together, we began to talk, and the more we talked, the more we got interested in each other's life. We discussed the latest news and the situation in the Soviet Union. My country was living through a difficult time, and Barb and Milton were very sympathetic with my concern. I couldn't help worrying, because the situation in Russia at the time could have gotten out of control any minute. And I am glad the country went through the changes peacefully.

❋

I was speechless the morning Vera quietly told me that she was pregnant! I had never had children and had no idea what we would do if there were complications. I was quite shaken by the fact that I was going to be responsible for this mother-to-be for the next three months. In spite of Vera's protests, I immediately called for an appointment with my doctor, an OB/GYN specialist. Dr. Maura Welch offered her services free of charge and arranged for a sonogram. I had never seen one before and was absolutely fascinated, but Vera showed no emotion. I asked her, "Isn't this exciting to see your baby on the screen?" She answered, "Not really. This is America, and I expect miracles in America."

Another American cultural experience awaited Vera when a friend of one of the doctor's wives held a baby shower for her in their beautiful home. Vera protested when I told her about it, saying that in Russia they never held a shower until after the baby was born. In spite of her protests to me, I believe she enjoyed this American tradition and appreciated the many gifts for her baby-to-be.

All five ladies were beginning to smile by the time of Vera's baby shower.

Love, Vera

Comparing Cultures

I was happy to find out that my new friends both enjoyed reading and had a wonderful library at home (contrary to the general belief that Americans only read comics). As a student at University I had read a great number of both English and American authors, but those were mostly writers of the past (Dickens, Dreiser, Hemingway, O'Henry, etc.). Barb knew very little of them. I understood that we had been given to read only writers with the right ideas. Talking with Barb, I realized that I had missed a big part of American literature. I started to catch up with the modern American authors. We spent a big deal of time traveling in the car. Barb is a born storyteller, and while taking me to some distant place for a meeting, Barb would talk about her childhood or university years. I enjoyed those moments together. Barb said she did most of the talking, but I felt I was limited in word choice and couldn't make my stories sound nice. Now we've been friends for over 28 years, and I still enjoy Barb's wonderful stories.

During my three-month stay, I met thousands of people. Wherever we gave talks there were so many people that I simply couldn't remember them. But there were people we met several times and had some activities together, and I do remember them. Dr. Hart, an eye doctor, checked my eyesight and prescribed glasses. Jenny Barker invited me to her lesson of French at school, and we met several times after that, talking about American and Russian schools. Sam and Nancy Douglas were farmers and Milton's clients. I met them at a dinner and several years later, when I came to GC with my son, we spent a couple of most enjoyable days on their farm. It was fun to talk to Jimmie Ruth, Barb's friend.

Through our communications we found out that basically Americans and Russians were very much alike. We were mostly involved in our family lives and careers, enjoyed our children and worried about them being disagreeable or getting into trouble. We had friends and enjoyed their company. We loved our homes and enjoyed good food. We were interested in politics and didn't

Love, Vera

mind gossiping from time to time. We loved our countries and our cultures and history. Nevertheless, there were some differences which could be explained by different standards of life and social systems.

    I'd like to begin with homes. Unlike in Russia, people in America mostly live in houses. I don't remember seeing high-rises in that part of the country. I visited many homes and was surprised how comfortable they were. To tell the truth, at the very beginning the houses looked like palaces to me. I had never been to such nice houses before. In Russia the majority of people in cities lived (and still do) in blocks of flats. People didn't own their flats; they rented from the government. The rent was very small, though. That was the good point. Very few people had houses, and those were very small houses with no running water or gas; they had to carry water from the well and heat their houses with wood. I remember, people living in houses would even wish they'd lived in flats, especially with such insignificant rent. I lived with my granny in a five-story block of flats. There were three rooms in our apartment but there was a neighbor who lived in one room, and we shared the bathroom and the kitchen. We were lucky, though. He lived with his girl-friend somewhere else and would occasionally come when they had an argument. A lot of people were less fortunate and had to share their apartments with several other families. The kitchen in such apartments would be crammed with tables, and there were lines to get to the bathroom. Thank God, apartments like that are rare now, as people were given a chance to buy new apartments.

    I visited many homes in GC, and they all looked grand to me. McMinimy's was the best of course. I started thinking of it as home, especially as its owners made me feel at home. I had my own bedroom and a bathroom, and there were certain places in the house I particularly liked; I enjoyed sitting in the kitchen and watching squirrels play in the back yard. Barb is a great lover of birds; she kept the binoculars on the kitchen table to watch the birds. But I loved squirrels – they were so playful and fun to watch. I would sometimes do the contrary to what Barb told me to do. For instance, if she said, "Let the dogs out or the squirrels will frighten the birds from their feeders, " I would keep the dogs in and have fun watching the squirrels.

    Another wonderful place in the house was the sitting room with a fireplace and lots of books. We spent many evenings there talking about books and life. I still remember those peaceful evenings very well. It is since those wonderful evenings that I started to dream of living in a house; and although Andy and I now live in a three-room apartment, which is all ours, I still have a hope that some day I'll live in a small house of my own and enjoy cold winter nights knitting or reading in front of a fireplace. Strangely, though, most people in Russia don't mind living in apartments, saying that having a house is too much of a chore.

In GC all people lived in houses and all families had a car or two. Nowadays there are lots of cars in Russia, but in those days it struck me as a luxury. Only two people in the apartment house where I lived owned a car; one of them was a disabled war veteran — the government provided veterans with small cars. I enjoyed traveling in comfortable American cars along smooth roads, especially when it was the only means of transport in GC. Barb and Milton often had to leave their office to take me to some place, and it made me feel guilty. So, I said I could take a bus. They laughed — there were no buses in GC. There weren't even taxis! It was a new experience to live in a city without any public transport — whether by bus or train or metro. Our family had never owned a car. I guess it was hard for my American friends to understand how one can survive without a car. Later, when I visited schools, I noticed that there were far too many cars in the parking lots to be the teachers'. Can you imagine how surprised I was to learn that they were the students'? In Russia there were no school buses at that time. There was no need for them; all children went to the nearest school! And since most people lived in apartment blocks, students lived within walking distance from their school. Now there are quite a lot of private schools and they bring their students in school buses. Apart from giving talks at schools, I visited a few lessons and was surprised to see how relaxed the students were and how little work they did during the lesson. In Russia students were kept busy throughout the lessons and teachers worked hard to make everyone do their best.

There was another surprise waiting for us in the shops. It was December, the time when in the USSR we could buy a limited choice of fruits and vegetables (apples and oranges, potatoes, onions, garlic, cabbage, carrots and beets). And there were lots and lots of vegetables and fruits in the Dillons grocery store, many of which we saw for the first time. Now of course we have all possible kinds of fruits and vegetables all the year round, but at that time it seemed miraculous to us.

We also visited lots of churches, both in GC and in many other places, and I liked it — much more than going to schools. I was surprised to find so many churches in one place and to learn that although they were all Christian, they were different: Methodist, Congregational, Catholic, Baptist, etc. As far as I remember, there were more than 30 churches in GC. Well, my hometown with the population of one million had only two churches! Both of them were

Love, Vera

Orthodox. There were just a few Orthodox churches in Moscow and those were closely supervised by the authorities. (There are more than 800 Orthodox churches in Moscow now, and they are not enough; you can hardly get in on big holidays. More mosques, synagogues, Catholic and Protestant churches have been built in the last twenty years.) I was amazed at the great number of churches and their diversity. I tried hard to understand the differences between, say, Methodist and Baptist churches but failed.

Barb and Milton took me to the Community Congregational Church, and I was very happy. I liked going to the Sunday School before the service. It was more like a book group, though. I remember we discussed a book on psychology. We were given a task before the lesson to read certain chapters, and then we discussed the material during the lesson. It wasn't the kind of activity I would expect to do in church, but I liked it, although I sometimes wasn't quite ready for the lesson – as I said, I was terribly pressed for time. It was one day in the church that I understood the words Milton would often repeat: "Vera, you don't know how you've changed our lives." Of course, I thought I had brought so many problems – taking me to places, entertaining guests at their home, visiting so many functions. But it was not quite that. Once in the church a man who was a banker was speaking to Milton and kept complaining about his problems. He repeated the word "problems" quite a few times, so Milton said, smiling: "If you want to know about problems, speak to Vera. She can tell you all about problems." I understood that I had helped them to realize how lucky they were, living comfortably in a country with a steady political and economic situation. They said they had learned to count their blessings.

Going to church was a new experience, and little as I understood the service, I thoroughly enjoyed it. I remember I envied the visitors who had been brought up in the Christian tradition and could bring their children without the awareness that they did something antisocial. Thank God believers are not persecuted in Russia any longer!

The Russian Orthodox church and the American Christian church are quite different. In America it is more like a club where people would meet to discuss all kinds of issues, and they may have activities like parties or even sports. In Russia the service is very formal and people do not necessarily go to the same church. They may go to different churches, and the service will be exactly the same wherever they go. The church service is held every day in most places, and many hold two services a day.

Another activity I enjoyed was reading groups. Barb was a member of two groups, one in Sunday school, and they didn't discuss a religious book. There was another group where I participated. I had never done anything like that before. Of course, libraries would hold conferences on certain authors, but they were organized by some officials. I liked the idea of people doing something on their own accord. Here the people chose which books to read and what questions to discuss, and they did it on a regular basis. I think you are encouraged to read, and it disciplines you. On return I made a suggestion to my friends to get together and share our ideas about books but found no support. Of course, we read a lot and advise on what books to read, but it isn't quite the same.

Well, the very phenomenon of the groups was new to us. There were all kinds of groups. Some of them seemed very strange, like the group that was preoccupied with finding the ways to make the preparation of breakfast easier and faster. They met regularly, shared ideas and demonstrated their skills. And they even took minutes of their discussions. I was bewildered. Why should they spend so much time on finding out how to do something faster when they could use this time on actually doing it? I understood the idea only later. People in small places had more spare time, and in America everyday life was much more relaxing (for example, they didn't have to waste time standing in lines), and they looked for ways to get themselves involved in activities, which would give them an extra chance to meet friends and enjoy their company. Some groups were just great!

We visited several groups in churches. There were women with small kids and even babies. They did some needlework. While they were working and visiting, somebody "on duty" would keep an eye on the children. I thought it was great. I tried to implement this idea when I returned home and had Andy. It worked for some time and gave us a chance to get some free time for ourselves. But it didn't become a regular practice and, when the children reached the age of three, mothers chose to send them to day care. I must admit that day care centers are very popular in Russia. And most of them are quite good. I have never liked the idea of leaving my son for the whole day in a company of about twenty kids, though. I believe small children should stay with their parents most of the time. They certainly feel much more comfortable at home.

As for handicrafts, I was mostly fascinated by quilt-making. We used to have this craft in old Russia, but they never made such elaborate quilts, so I was very interested in seeing as many quilts as I could. I visited all the local museums and quilt groups. I could never stop wondering how women actually did it — it must take so much practice and time. And artistic skill, of course. It is strange that Americans don't appreciate those old quilts they inherited from

Love, Vera

their grandmothers. I saw some wonderful handmade quilts in second-hand shops being sold for a few dollars, when that could be a work of months or even years. My friend Barb has a wonderful quilt that covers "my" bed — the most elaborate combination of gentle blue colors and patterns. I'm glad the craft is finding a new interest in Russia now, although I don't dare to start doing it.

Another reason for my interest in local museums was that one could see personal things, like somebody's great-grandmother's wedding dress or a table cloth — something you don't see in Russian museums. I guess Russians just didn't have enough room in their flats to keep those dear old things. It's too bad — it helps to feel the never-ending stream of lives of your family.

Having made an acquaintance with all those groups and clubs, I came to the conclusion that there were so many places to spend your time because you do have spare time. I don't mean Americans work less, no. That was another surprise — how much Americans work. Milton was an example. He worked long hours every day and practically every weekend. During those three months, I remember just a few days he didn't work. It was Christmas, when we went to Colorado Springs, and maybe another two or three days. I didn't understand his enthusiasm at the time, because in the Soviet Union everyone worked for the government and got a salary that hardly depended on how much you worked. We didn't have private companies then. Now there are a lot of self-employed people who are ready to work as much as they can to make their business profitable. As for Americans having more leisure time, I think that's because their everyday life is much easier and more relaxed. They have cars and can get to places fast.

What is more, parents in Russia had to spend a lot of time helping their kids with homework — kids get a lot of home tasks every day and it is a must that they do it. Working mothers (and almost all women worked at the time) had to divide their time between cooking and helping their children with lessons. You had to be very organized to fit in some leisure activities.

Besides, there is a great choice of ready made food, or one can eat at a restaurant at reasonable prices. While in America for the first time, I was surprised how often people could go out. In Russia it would have cost a fortune!

By the way, the first McDonald's in Moscow had been opened just before my trip to the USA. It was a great event and got a lot of coverage in the media. People would spend hours in the line to get in — it was fast and had more or less reasonable prices. I never had time to stand in that line, so when we just started to plan our trip I thought: "That will be my chance to try that wonderful fast food." Alas, Barb and Milton had other preferences, and I was too shy to ask. Once Barb said she was very busy and we would simply have to have lunch in a McD. I tried hard not to show that I was over the moon at the perspective. We drove to a McD, but right in front of it Barb said: "No, I am NOT taking you there," and we went somewhere else, away from fast food. I realized that I had lost my last and only chance. So when I came home I didn't have a chance to boast about being acquainted with famous American fast food. "Barb took me to other restaurants, much better ones," I would say and saw disappointment in people's eyes. Only eight years later, when I came to the USA with my son, did I have that chance. Andy would get real naughty in regular restaurants where you have to wait for your food, and we just had to go to fast food restaurants. I overheard Barb saying to Milton, "Please be patient; it's only for one more month. Just think, only a month of fast food and you won't have to eat it for the rest of your life." Then I understood how much sacrifice my dear friends were ready to make for me. Thank you, dears.

Barb and Milton like going out to eat, but they also have wonderful meals at home. Milton used to visit different cookery classes and was a member of a dinner group. They interested themselves in ethnic cuisines and wouldn't miss a chance to have a Russian dinner in our house. (I say "our" – that's how I felt in the McMinimy house, quite at home, thanks to a wonderful relationship we had established.) The plan was to give each American member of the group a task to make one dish and those dishes would make a great Russian dinner. I gave out recipes to people. Cooking some dishes was like doing a quest: people could only guess what kind of dish they would get. For example, one woman was to make kisel – something in between a drink and a dessert, prepared with berries, water and starch. When she came, she asked me shyly, "Does it look like kisel to you?" Another woman cooked Russian borscht. According to the recipe, she needed neck bones to make it, but where could she get those, if there are no bones sold in supermarkets at all? Well, she was clever and went straight to the meat-packing plant. People there were quite surprised to have somebody wanting neck bones. She found every single ingredient for her borscht, but she boiled all the vegetables whole, so we had to chop them on the spot. I am glad people had so much fun cooking their meals, and they had lots of stories to share during our Russian dinner. It was fun!

No wonder people in America are so fond of cookery classes – you can find any ingredient you want in the nearest supermarket. First, when I heard: "Let's cook this or that." I thought: "How could you decide what to cook, when you don't have the ingredients for it? Suppose you won't find what you need?"

Love, Vera

I certainly took people by surprise. In Russia, however, you first took into consideration what you could get and only then planned your meals. People wouldn't understand how one can have a choice buying flour or sugar. It was just, "Buy some sugar, please," as there was one kind of sugar.

I thought I wouldn't be able to describe American shops when I am back in Russia, so Milton decided to take some pictures at the Dillons grocery store to make it easier for me. We went to the shop and had taken a few pictures when a man came up and asked what we were doing. He said they didn't want anybody to take pictures because they may be used by their competitors to help with ideas for the layout. Well, Milton said that for where I was going they were useless, as there was nothing to lay out in the Soviet Union in 1991! Now I am very glad we have a great variety of foods on offer and people can cook fancy meals. But at that time American supermarkets seemed almost unreal — how can it be that you could get anything you wanted without struggling in a line?

In Russia prices before 1991 were always the same. Whatever shop you went to in any part of the country, things cost exactly the same. Prices didn't change for decades. I still remember our amazement when we learned about discounts and sales!

Mac posing in the bakery section of Garden City's local grocery store, Dillons.

There was a Walmart nearby, and Valya and I would stroll along the aisles bewildered at the great variety of what seemed to us the same product, say flour or milk. The shop looked like a whole district in a town with everything man would ever want. By the way, eventually we found something which wasn't on offer — it was egg powder. When we told our American friends about it, they asked: "Why would anyone ever need egg powder?" Well, the answer was: "In case you can't find eggs in the shops!" I am so glad we are past those times! Once, when I had only stayed for a few weeks and hadn't been to shops on my own, Barb asked me to buy napkins. It was urgent, because we were expecting guests. I got hysterical: I imagined myself alone in those jungles trying to find that certain brand of napkins she was used to buying. Well, I bought the right kind, of course, but I still remember how nervous I was shopping by myself for the first time.

After a while I got used to good service and the outstanding variety of everything in American shops and even became picky. I remember once I wanted to buy mushrooms, and they had to be really small mushrooms. It seemed to me that the mushrooms in the shop were not small enough, so I asked a man there to find exactly the right size. The man telephoned the other Dillons to ask if they had mushrooms of the right size. I was impressed by the service, but Barb was even more impressed by how demanding I had become. I must say that Americans are lucky to have such great service. Shop assistants are always nice and ready to do anything to oblige you. They can be friendly and helpful without making a special effort. In Russia of that time we were not used to being treated especially nice in shops or restaurants. "You don't like it, you can go anywhere else." I am very happy to see that the attitude of people to their customers is changing. We now have a choice where to go, and the shops and restaurants are private, so the owners certainly won't have rude staff to scare customers away.

The original arrangement for our stay was: we spend three months in Garden City and then the kind people of GC share us with Chanute, another Kansas town 300 miles east of GC, for three more months. On the way to Chanute we were to stay in Hesston for a week. For me it meant that I would have to have a baby in America, but I didn't like that idea from the start. I set to leave earlier than planned – early enough to give birth in Russia. Many people in GC advised me to stay and have the baby in America. They would give different reasons why I should do that. Bonnie Talley's argument was the funniest: "If your son is born in America, he can be the president of the USA one day." Well, of course she was a politician, as Barb used to say. Some women would argue that the situation in the Soviet Union was bad and it wasn't safe to rely on the medicine there at the time. That was true, and we got news that there were shortages of everything, medicines included.

One day Bonnie took me to the local hospital to demonstrate how well everything worked there. Indeed, I was impressed by what I saw. In Russia, once a pregnant woman got to hospital, she became a prisoner: they feared infection and regarded every visitor as the sure cause of disease for you or your baby. So, for your sake they would keep you in hospital at least for a week after birth (if everything went well), and then the only way to visit with your family would be through the window or by writing letters. (There were no cell phones back then.) It had some advantages, though — I still have letters my family wrote to me while I was in hospital.

So imagine my surprise when they let me visit the wards, and I saw relatives there visiting with women who had just given birth, and their new babies were also there! I was even able to see some premature babies and how they were supervised. I think Bonnie was determined to persuade me to stay and give birth in GC and made sure they demonstrated how safe it would be for me. In the SU, even if they let people visit their relatives in the hospital (never women with their babies, though), they made them change their shoes and wear special white gowns. Now a lot of things have changed, and fathers are allowed to be present while the baby is born.

Also, one old lady had a talk with me, trying to make me stay. Her strong argument was that she was very experienced at baby care, since she had five children and numerous grandchildren. She definitely wanted her share of adventure and urged me to move to her house, as Barb seemed inexperienced to her mind, while if I moved to her place I would be perfectly safe. Well, I guess I disappointed a lot of people with my determination to go home. I am so sorry; I loved them all, but I was ready to go home.

Dr. Welch had advised Vera that she should not travel after the seventh month of her pregnancy (around March 1st), so she was planning to return to Moscow with Ira and Tim around the first of February. Several Garden Citians tried to convince her to stay and have her baby in the U.S., even offering to pay for the costs; but Vera would not hear of this, insisting that her child MUST be born in Russia and be a Russian citizen. She had entered my life as a stranger but had become a dear friend, and I talked her into staying one more month.

Hesston, Kansas

The three months went quickly, and I was ready to leave Garden City. First we were going to Hesston, a small city near Wichita. Although Barb was to meet me a week later, we were both very sad, because we knew that once I left America we wouldn't see each other for a long time, if ever. People in Hesston gave us a very warm welcome. Our activities were pretty much the same: we talked to various groups — school children, clubs, church groups, teachers, businessmen — and learned more about Americans. People were very kind and, as perhaps in any small place, were very enthusiastic.

Somebody suggested throwing a party — a Russian dinner for the whole city. The organizers had sent out a lot of invitations, and we were to make enough food for the people who would come. There was a small entrance fee, so we were able to earn a little money. We decided to make meat dumplings. A huge amount of meat was bought, we made the dough and began two days of work. One woman was making borscht while the other three of us were making dumplings — non-stop for two days, until we had more than 2,000 dumplings! For me it was quite a challenge because I was seven months pregnant. I guess this might be the reason why my son's favorite dish is meat dumplings. The evening was fun; people said they liked the food, and we were very relieved to hear that.

There were two more memorable events in Hesston — a baby shower and shopping. I had two baby showers in America, one in GC and one in Hesston, both very pleasurable. In Russia there is a tradition to give presents and buy things for the baby only after it is born. I guess the superstition dates back to those times when people believed in evil spirits and wanted to chase them away from the baby to be born by pretending that there was no baby at all. I must admit that I was quite apprehensive before the first baby shower, but then I thought if Americans regularly have baby showers and their babies are born healthy, it was safe for me. However, once in Russia I followed the general tradition — we hadn't bought anything before my son was born, although buying even simple things for babies was a problem. I was given a lot during those American baby showers, but, unfortunately I had to leave most of those things behind because of the weight of my luggage.

Baby shower for Vera in Hesston, Kansas, in March of 1991.

Another event I remember was shopping. In Hesston I stayed with LeAnn and Stan Clark, and I was lucky again, for they made my stay a very pleasurable event.

LeAnn said she was fond of shopping and took us to some outlets. It was quite an experience! We had never been to such huge shops before, and with so many bargains! Like LeAnn said, we shopped till we dropped. And, surprisingly, I enjoyed it. In Russia at that time, shopping meant finding things you needed, and, if you were lucky to find something, you had to wait in a long line. Of course, I hated shopping there.

Vera with her Hesston host family, Stan and LeAnn Clark.

A Farewell With Little Hope

By the end of February our friendship had deepened so much that I could not bear to send my pregnant friend on that long train trip to Washington, D.C., by herself, so I decided to travel with her. I met Vera in Hesston, and we drove to Kansas City and spent the night with my brother and his wife. The next morning we made a short visit to the Kansas City Art museum before going to the train station, and she commented on how impressed she was with the art on display. She seemed surprised that we had paintings done by some of the most highly regarded artists from Europe. I was glad she had not left the U.S. without seeing something besides the small rural towns of southwestern Kansas.

Vera had been scheduled for so many talks and activities during her time in Garden City that it seemed we never had enough free time to talk with each other. We were both looking forward to this last chance to visit during our 25-hour train trip, and I believe we talked every waking minute. Our small sleeping compartment on the train had barely enough room for two people to stand next to each other. There was no way to sit comfortably on the bottom bunk bed and talk, so we found empty seats in another car and settled into them — until the next stop. That's when the conductor gave us a chewing-out for being in someone's reserved seats and banished us to our sleeper or the lounge car. I had tried to make this trip as pleasant as possible for my pregnant friend and was embarrassed that I hadn't understood the rules, leaving us with no comfortable place to sit for our long train trip. At least we had beds for sleeping.

Love, Vera

As we approached the outskirts of Washington, D.C., my heart grew heavy. The daughter of a Garden City friend met us at the train station and stayed with Vera until her plane left the next day for Moscow. We promised we would write to each other as we hugged goodbye, but I couldn't hold back my tears. (This was before the internet; letters took more than two weeks, and she had no telephone.) I was certain I would never see my Russian friend again.

The farewell journey on the train to Washington, D.C., with Barb was delightful and painful at the same time. Delightful because we enjoyed each other's company, and sad because we didn't know if we would ever meet again. We both remembered decades of Cold War when our nations were separated by politicians, and we couldn't be certain about the future.

Well, thank God we have met quite a few times since then and have been communicating both by telephone and Skype. And before Skype we wrote letters, of course. Barb wrote letters full of motherly concern about Andy and me and my family ("You are all in our thoughts more than you can know."), and Milton sent letters to little Andy with fatherly advice to: "be good and mind your wise mother." Other friends would also write and even give practical advice.

At the airport, when I was boarding the Russian plane, I felt people were staring at me in surprise. There was one TV presenter who came up to me and said: "What do you think you are doing? Every woman dreams of giving birth in America. You are losing your only chance to let your child become an American citizen. Besides, it is not safe in the SU now."

Perhaps it was selfish of me, but I couldn't wait to be home with all my relatives. I am sure the American Embassy put some mark, something like "stupid", in my file because I have never had problems with getting a visa, even when they were especially strict and denied visas to many people.

When I came back to Russia I was attacked with questions by both relatives and friends. And I did have a lot of stories to tell. People listened apprehensively — it was hard for them to believe that Americans, who had been seen as enemies for so long, turned out friendly and nice.

DIFFICULT TIMES: A CRUMBLING SOVIET UNION

Vera returned to her home near Moscow the first week of March of 1991, and I became more and more anxious as I watched the news and waited to hear from her. On March 17th the Soviet Union held a referendum on the preservation of the Soviet Union as a federation of equal republics; and although the referendum passed, a number of the republics began breaking away from the Soviet Union to form independent nations.

When her first letter finally arrived in April, she told me that there had been complications with her pregnancy shortly after her arrival home and she had been in the hospital for ten days.

They don't let families come and see us — they are afraid of infections. I dream of the time when they let me get up and I'll be able to go to the telephone and talk to family and friends. If I could get out of bed, I would talk to Sergi and Mother through the window. They bring me things every day to eat. I don't know where they get fruit and even caviar. I guess they have to pay a fortune for it and by the time I get out of here we'll be completely ruined.

The State shops are as empty as they were. The prices for some things are up to ten times more than they were when I left, and that wasn't official price reform. They will officially raise prices on the 1st of April (April Fools' Day) and I don't know from what level. But there is little hope that food or goods will be easier to get. But I think that if things don't get worse we'll make it. They even give me (as I'm pregnant) a monthly food package (eight pounds of meat, some fish, butter, oil and three pounds of cereals).

Love, Vera

> *In political life there is little change. They didn't let much freedom on TV and radio, but the newspapers publish anything. We had a referendum on Sunday, but I don't know the results yet. I hope the relations between our countries won't change to the worse at least, and I'll see you here. I feel so frustrated that I can't communicate with you.*

A few weeks later I received my second letter from her. She was out of the hospital.

> *Today, for the first time I went to the shops — and it was an awful disappointment. There is nothing for babies but bonnets, and those are very expensive. The prices are awfully high — three and more times higher than before. But we know the prices only from newspapers — there is not much in the shops. In some cities people are on strike, but here everything is calm. It's amazing how much patience our people have.*
>
> *There is a good though old joke (comes from Brezhnev time): An American delegation on human rights comes to Moscow. They say to Brezhnev that there is no freedom in the USSR because nobody can go on strike. So Brezhnev orders to arrange a strike at a very big automobile plant. The boss gathers the workers and announces that they will get twice smaller wages. The next day everybody works as usual. So they warn people that for less wages they will have to work more hours — nothing happens, everybody comes to work. Next time they gather people and announce that they are going to hang every fourth one of them. One worker says, "Can I ask a question?" "Yes, please." — "Should we bring the ropes or will you provide them?" — That is the psychology of our people. They are so tired of shortages that they hope there will be something in the shops even for these prices.*

Andy was born on April 24th, and Vera's next few letters were filled with optimism. Food was more available during the summer and she had cereal and milk for her baby boy. She wrote that the situation in Moscow was calm, with ... *battles only taking place in Parliaments. Perhaps we are becoming a civilized nation.*

That summer Mac and I worried about all of our Moscow friends as we nervously watched the news reports of the upheaval in the Soviet Union. Abkhazia and Transnistria (provinces of Ukraine and Moldova) and the three Baltic republics (Lithuania, Estonia, and

Latvia) had declared their independence from the USSR in 1990, and Georgia became independent in April of 1991.

In her letter of August 14th she wrote:

> We have terrible inflation now, Rubles cost nothing but dollars are very expensive. It's a pity that we teachers get 15-20 dollars monthly. For one dollar, you can buy one kilo (more than two pounds) of meat or one-half kilo of fruit or berries or two kilos of cottage cheese or ten liters (a liter is roughly a quart) of milk. Prices in the shops are even lower. For poor Americans, I would recommend to come here and live in Russia. They can live comfortably for 30 to 50 dollars a month (if they don't need clothes or shoes, of course — they wouldn't find such things here).
>
> I don't watch TV at all and sometimes hear the radio so I don't follow political events closely. Yeltsin made a law that forbids party activity in enterprises and institutions but communists resist. They try to assure us that we won't survive without them. But thanks to them, we already learned to live without decent food and clothes and many other things so I think we'll be all right without party bosses too. The governments have changed but it is a strange change: from Communists to Democrats but somehow it happened that all Democrats are former Communists and they talk nicely but have the same ways as before.

On August 19th, government members who were opposed to perestroika launched a coup. We fearfully followed the television coverage as military troops surrounded the Russian White House, their Parliament building. Large numbers of protesters gathered and we watched with relief as the troops defected and joined in the protests. (We learned later that two of our Russian visitors to Garden City, Valya and Tamara, participated in those protests.) Yeltsin climbed on top of a tank turret and made a memorable speech that rallied mass opposition to the coup, and by August 21st the coup leaders were arrested or had fled. Her much-awaited next letter finally arrived a few weeks later.

> On a Monday morning (Blue Monday indeed) we heard a nasty voice on the radio and understood at once what had happened. Such information and words were only too familiar for us during Brezhnev's time. That meant the end of every hope, power of KGB again, lots of propaganda, no communication

Love, Vera

with foreigners. So I thought I would never see you again. And I thought Andy would have to put up with communists like his parents. Those were awful days — we didn't have any information — only official announcements and lots of music and ballets on TV (Tchaikovsky's Swan Lake). They arrested progressive newspapers — and we only subscribe to these. For three days only communist press was allowed.

I made an important decision that I'd rather be a janitor (There are no communists among janitors.) than go back to work with communists again. Work in schools and with foreigners was considered by them to be an 'ideological front' — and I don't want to be a fighter of this front again. Thank God it is over and quick and I don't have to learn a new trade. They organized the coup like they did everything during the past 70 years — badly. (They say when they worked out their declaration they were drunk — which may be true.)

The danger of another coup still remains and there are quite a lot of people who supported them. The main damage that was done by the communist regime is to people. They succeeded in growing a new breed of people — unable to think. Minister of police promised order — and they didn't question him why he couldn't provide order without the coup, being a minister of police. Prime-Minister promised prosperity, but why didn't he do something before? It was a funny coup.

The important result of the victory of the Russian president is that the communist party was banned for a while and their property arrested. They have to learn to work underground. And it is funny that they say that it is non-democratic and discrimination and that all parties should have equal opportunities — they never gave any chances to others. They fight to survive now and support pro-communist regimes in Central Asia and some other Republics. Those Republics declared independence in haste not to let democratic forces develop there — and Russia gets surrounded by reactionary regimes, mostly Muslim, so we may have more Iraks.

Since Union government was located in Russia, Russians are blamed for discrimination and aggression. And now Russians are discriminated against in other Republics (and there are about 70 million Russians living 'abroad' — and quite a lot of non-Russians in Russia). Since the empire is falling apart, there is need to divide property. Republics believe that everything that is on their territory is theirs and what is in

Russia is common property of all nations and should be divided among all Republics. Thus Ukraine wouldn't sell us bread and fruit but demands oil and timber as always. Moreover, they insist that the borders should remain — and that is also unfair, since Stalin and Khrushchev gave lots of Russian lands to other Republics just like gifts.

So, the country is a great mess and we live right in the middle of it. I see this time you'll get a political letter — there is no room for anything else. Politics is really important for us now. We keep discussing things all the time, and I hope this will be of some interest to you.

We were indeed interested and deeply concerned about our new Russian friends as the political unrest in their country continued into the fall of 1991. The evening news told of soaring inflation (which reached 96% by the end of 1991). Food in the State shops became more scarce, and people were forced to buy from the black market at three or four times the cost in the shops. Consumers spent more and more time searching for supplies and standing in long queues. Wages were frozen, and the value of the ruble continued to drop. There was more incentive in looking for goods than working for rubles, so people stopped working. (They had a joke that the people pretended to work and the government pretended to pay them.)

Vera had been on a waiting list to get a telephone for a number of years. I was glad when she finally got her phone so we didn't have to depend on unreliable mail service to communicate. She and Andy and her mother and grandmother were sharing a two-bedroom apartment, and knowing that things were very difficult for them we sent cash with some of my letters. Soon those letters started getting "lost" somewhere along the way. After that we sent money only with someone who was traveling to Moscow and could give it to her in person. In her November letter she thanked us for sending money and said my letters ... *are arriving in about three weeks, which is not bad. Prices are going up every day. Food is getting terribly expensive, but sometimes we buy things unbelievably cheap, like the other day I bought a bicycle for Andy for 27 rubles, which is about 30 cents!*

I called Valya today, and her husband told me she was "in the line". She wanted to buy vegetable oil and was lining for

Love, Vera

quite a long time (her number was 600) — but in vain. So when I talked to her later she was irritated and tired.

Our government is bad again. Government gets nominated and sounds quite enthusiastic for a while but then resigns. New government is nominated — and nobody is responsible for what happened to our economy. And it's a shame for the country with our resources to beg for money from other nations, but as I see it if you start falling down, you can't voluntarily stop the process, you have to fall right to the bottom and then begin to rise again. I only wish we would reach the bottom soon. My only wish is that war doesn't start — people become more and more hostile. It's dangerous to go out when it's dark, and it's dark very early — at 3:30 because of the unreasonable change to daylight savings time in October.

In Vera's next letter she wrote about the Russian holiday season.

The tradition is to have your apartment cleaned, all your debts paid, cook lots of food for this family holiday and spend the evening visiting or dancing. On New Year's Day we often cross-country ski or take a walk. I have a small New Year's tree with lights on it and a few presents below for Andy.

I guess you have problems with writing our address — I don't know in what country we live. It's definitely not the Soviet Union any more — but I can't say what you should write, because by the time your letter comes here it may be different again. Sometimes I think we live in a madhouse.

The leaders of Russia, Ukraine, and Belarus secretly met and declared the dissolution of the Soviet Union in early December, and a few weeks later Gorbachev met with Yeltsin and agreed to dissolve the Soviet Union. The Russian Federation took the Soviet Union's seat in the United Nations on December 24th, and the following day Gorbachev resigned and declared his office extinct. On the evening of December 26th, 1991, the Soviet flag was lowered from the Kremlin and replaced with the pre-revolutionary Russian flag. Yeltsin became both the prime minister and the president.

In January of 1992, Yeltsin removed price controls on most items in an effort to bring goods into the shops and create a market-based economy. This spurred inflation, which reached 2000% by the end the year. The government printed more money, and the value of the ruble declined. Then factories began paying workers "in kind", and a barter economy emerged.

Mail service to Moscow was non-existent in the spring of 1992, and the only letters I received from Vera were hand-carried by Americans who visited Moscow and mailed them to us when they returned to the U.S. The next letter I received included a photo of her with little Andy and was written on January 13th, Russia's "old New Year".

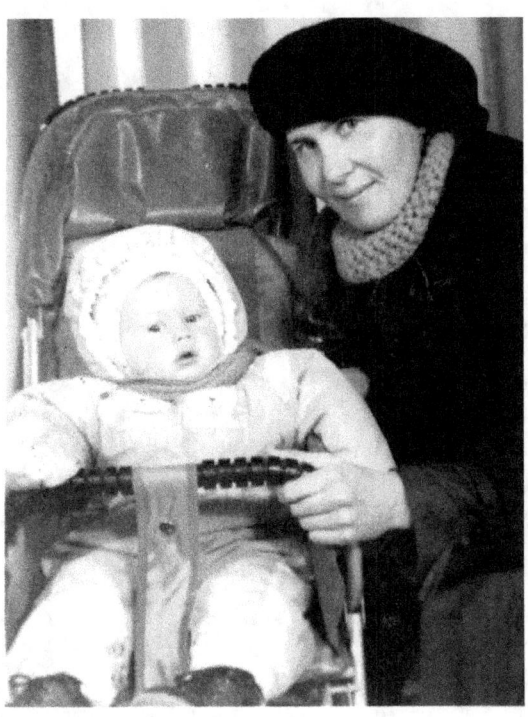

Baby Andy in the snowsuit given to Vera at Garden City's baby shower.

We'll not celebrate it this year, or rather will celebrate by going to bed early. Holiday season is not very gay this year, hearing all the sad news on radio and TV about wars in the Caucasus and the economic situation in Russia. I spent the day shopping (or rather running from one shop to another) and there is nothing in the shops. They assured us that after prices had gone up we'd have a lot of goods — another lie. So I am in a bad mood. The government promises it will be better by summer. I wish to God it were true.

Since the mail was unreliable, I began calling her once a month. We were making plans to visit her in July, so she arranged through a friend to get us an official invitation so we could get our visas. I was becoming quite excited about our upcoming trip but extremely worried about our Moscow friends. The very limited news we heard about Russia told only about the government's instability and the failing economy.

Love, Vera

First Impressions — 1992

The day finally arrived when Mac and I made the five-hour drive to Denver and spent the night near the airport. The next morning we began our flight to New York and then through seven more time zones to Moscow's international airport.

The terminal appeared to be in the middle of a forest and was surrounded by old concrete walls that were obviously in need of repair. This was Moscow, the capital of Russia, and we were surprised to see no other planes within sight either from the air or parked near the terminal. I watched through the window as we waited to deplane and saw a man standing beside two steel-wheeled baggage carts similar to those used by the railroads in the early 20th century. As we started going across the tarmac to the doors of the terminal, he grabbed one cart with each hand and began walking toward our plane to unload our luggage. It felt like we had stepped back in time.

There was an eerie quiet as we walked past soldiers carrying rifles and joined the other passengers in one of the four lines at customs. The travelers around us spoke to each other in whispers or not at all, and the near-silence made me feel extremely nervous. The young men behind the counters looked bored and did not speak; they moved very slowly as they solemnly checked our passports. I breathed a sigh of relief as my passport was finally given back to me and I moved away from the counter. As we started toward the fence about 50 feet away, I saw Vera waving to us from the other side. Bonnie Talley had traveled from Garden City to Moscow a week earlier and was standing by Vera and Valya, and they greeted us with flowers, balloons, and an American flag. Their smiling faces and warm greetings were so very welcome after the strain of getting through customs!

Love, Vera

Vera's brother, Sasha, drove us on the four-lane road from the airport to Moscow, weaving through traffic at break-neck speed. When we got to Moscow, he stopped to ask for directions from a policeman directing traffic at a busy intersection. Then he drove to a farmers' market where vendors from Georgia, Armenia, and Azerbaijan were selling fresh tomatoes, peaches, apricots, etc. We saw no smiles, and people looked past us, rather than meeting our eyes.

Our next stop was to buy bread at a State shop. The few shelves inside contained meat, baby food, baked goods and sweets, and most people were queued at the meat counter. The display case was not refrigerated. Chickens on display were plucked and without heads — not at all what we were used to at home. After standing in the queue to prepay for the bread (where an abacus was used to calculate the cost), Sasha took the receipt to another queue to pick up his loaves of white and brown bread.

Sasha continued speeding through Moscow traffic, passing cars, buses, trolleys and numerous trucks. The lack of landscaping or maintenance in this capital city surprised me. I was beginning to realize the severity of Russia's declining economy. On the way to Vera's town, we learned that Sasha didn't have a driver's license. He was a very aggressive driver, and I noticed Mac gripping the door handle and pushing his feet against the floor board. Vera and I were visiting in the back seat, and she didn't seem aware of how nervous Mac and I were. At one point we turned off the main road, and Sasha had to drive more slowly in order to veer around numerous large potholes. It was a very hot day, and we passed a man walking along the road in his shorts and shoes, carrying his suit and shirt.

Vera's apartment was on the 4th floor (left balcony) — we were directly above her.

Vera's apartment building looked similar to countless others we had seen along the way. The same design had been used throughout the Soviet Union during the 1960s: concrete block, five stories, no elevator.

Her mother was holding Andy and beaming as she opened the door of their fourth-floor apartment. Vera translated for her mother while we ate some fruit and a Danish. Then she led us up the concrete stairs to her friend's fifth floor apartment directly above her own. She had arranged for us stay there during the next two weeks while her friends were tending their garden in the country. Many Russians prefer to grow their own vegetables because of the high costs of vegetables in the stores and bazaars and the widespread belief in excessive use of agrochemicals for food found in markets and grocery stores. They also enjoy having a connection to the land while escaping the heat of the city during hot summers.

All of the apartments had the same efficient room layout: a 12' by 24' living room with a balcony, two 10' x 20' bedrooms, a tiny kitchen

Kitchen of the 5th floor apartment where we stayed.

Notice the single long faucet serving both the tub and sink.

Love, Vera

and a bath. The kitchen had vinyl flooring, a gas oven-range, and a 1960s-era refrigerator, while the other rooms had beautiful hardwood parquet floors and large windows. Instead of closets, each bedroom had a spacious wooden wardrobe.

Vera provided us with a coffee pot and plenty of coffee, fresh eggs, fresh fruit, corn flakes, cheese, milk purchased from a local farmer, kefir (like yogurt), and bread for breakfast. I must admit we were a little concerned about that cotton stopper in the bottle of raw milk. She had suggested we relax over breakfast in our apartment and come down to her apartment in mid-morning, but we had not adjusted to the time difference and woke up around three or four in the morning. As spoiled Americans, we were not used to sleeping without air conditioning, and sounds from nearby apartments and mosquitoes found their way to our bedroom.

When Barb and Milton first came to Russia in the summer of 1992, I guess their visit was as exciting and adventurous as mine to America, except they knew the people they were going to stay with. And they had a very special mission — they were to become my son's godparents.

Before their arrival I was very nervous. And I had all the reasons to be: first they couldn't possibly stay at our place because it was just two rooms and a kitchen in an old five-story block of flats. I was very happy when my neighbors from an apartment upstairs said they would be away for the summer and I could have their apartment. Of course it wasn't quite the type of place Barb and Milton were used to staying at, but being very polite people, they didn't complain.

Another reason for my worry was food. Although the situation on the market was much better than in 1990-91 when one had to stand in line for staples like bread or milk, the choices were still limited. I was worried that Barb and Milton would find our food too plain and would stay hungry most of the time — I was wrong; they were very enthusiastic to try Russian dishes (and also drinks) and seemed to enjoy them. After their visit Barb wrote:

> Everyone spoiled us with such good meals as mushrooms, soups, meats, fresh salad, wonderful vegetables from so many gardens, and that unforgettable Russian bread! How did you manage so many good foods prepared by you and Mother and

Olga and other friends? And the melons and jams and honey, and cakes, and wines and champagne!

❈

It was still early when we finished breakfast, so Mac and I went for a walk. We followed a path past a school with several boarded up windows and arrived at a four-lane road with rows of tall apartment buildings and rather austere shops. Since we had no sense of direction and needed landmarks to find our way back, we stood and watched for a while before returning.

An olive-drab canvas-back truck stopped, and a woman holding a scale stepped out of the back and set up a small stand. Then she unloaded a few boxes of fruit and vegetables and began arranging her produce on the stand. A line immediately began forming. As the truck pulled away, we could see several more women with scales sitting by boxes in the back.

Canvas back trucks were often used as delivery trucks.

Vera and Sasha were waiting when we returned. It was July 24th, Mac's birthday, and Vera had informed us the evening before that Andy was going to be baptized that day and that we were to be his godparents! The priest had refused to allow this at first because we were not Russian Orthodox. When he found out we were members of a Congregational church, he said that was as far away from Orthodoxy as you could get. Vera had argued with him until he agreed we could participate if Vera's father was also a godparent.

Sasha drove us to the church, with Mac again risking his life in the front seat as the car sped through traffic. Vera's parents, Bonnie, Valya, Ira and Tim were waiting at God's Mother's Icon of Tihvin Church. Since this was one of a very few churches in the Moscow area that had not been either destroyed, converted to a museum, or used for storage by the Soviets, it was in continual use seven days a week and had more than one service going on at a time. It was a Wednesday, and there were weddings, funerals, and baptisms scheduled throughout the day; a wedding party was gathering on the steps as we arrived. We walked up the enclosed staircase and saw five more wedding parties waiting inside. Old women in headscarves stood just inside the entry while a priest performed a service for the dead. A man in black was kneeling, then bowed prostrate to the ground. Vera's grandmother had died earlier that year, and she heard the priest announce her grandmother's name.

Icons and frescoes covered every inch of the walls and ceilings of the sanctuary. There were no pews. An elderly woman wearing black moved cloth-draped lecterns here and there, and people moved about lighting candles and looking at icons. It felt very organic. At the far end of the church we observed a service in process, and an a-cappella quintet dressed in street clothes was singing. People stood as the priest dipped a big brush in water and snapped the brush with a wrist motion to spray drops of water on them. The singers got wet and laughed quietly. Each of the worshipers stepped forward to touch his or her head to the priest's cross and then kiss it. We walked down the steps to the lower level and joined two young couples waiting with their children. The room had a high ceiling and a pillar in the middle. On one wall were verses written in Russian and paintings of Orthodox crosses on either side of a large painting of Jesus being baptized by John the Baptist. A large urn for infant baptisms and a tiled, sunken tub for older children and adults stood near the center of the room. Notes from a journal that Mac kept during the first few days we were in Russia give the best description of our next hour:

The priest goes to a wardrobe to get wrist bands and a white robe, saying a blessing as he puts them on and then begins the service. The godparents are given long, thin candles and they are lit. The priest reads. Vera's father is holding Andy and reads the verses on the wall. They are written in old Russian, and he has a hard time reading them. He is reading them for all the godparents and is prompted by the priest. We turn toward the painting on the wall — a godmother who is next to me turns me around. (She helps me to stay with the ceremony.) After a while the priest leads the godparents around the pillar three times. Then he dips a brush in colored water, goes up to the three children and blows twice in their faces. Using the little brush, he makes a cross on each forehead, eye, chin, chest, hand and foot of the children.

Three lit candles are on the urn. The baby girl is about six months old and is immersed first. She is held horizontal over the large urn and the priest covers her nose and mouth with his hand and lowers her three times. Then she is given to her parents, who have a towel. The older boy (about six or seven years old) is taken to the sunken tub. I can't see the ritual — blocked by the pillar.

The priest begins the baptismal service for the three children.

Next is Andy. The priest takes him, and Andy is not happy. He resists the priest by holding onto Vera's father. Finally the priest has Andy — and into the urn he goes, three times. The priest works. Andy doesn't offer much resistance the first time, but he's crying loudly and trying to get free the next two times. His face turns red, and water is splashed everywhere and one candle goes out. Finally, the priest gives Andy to his grandfather, and Vera's mother towels him dry.

Then more chanting. A white baptismal cloth is put on each child and the priest places a cross around each child's neck. More chanting. My candle is getting low, and I am worried that it may not last. Andy's father puts out his candle and gives it to

Love, Vera

Fifteen-month old Andy is dipped into the urn face first.

Barb so he can handle Andy. The godmother next to me breaks off a small piece of wax from hers and gives it to me to give to Vera's father. I see that it is urgent that he have at least part of a candle. He doesn't seem to understand either, but he takes it. It's times like this to be reverent/respectful because I could tell that to the godmother of the oldest child this was a commitment!

Now we go upstairs to the left side of the church. The priest takes the baby girl, carries her to the Icon and touches her head to it, always chanting. He gives her back to her parents and takes the older child and Andy into a room behind the icon and comes out a door on the other side. He chants continuously, with Andy protesting loudly throughout the whole ceremony. He then lectures the godparents about our responsibilities (in Russian, of course), and the baptism concludes.

I bought a few icons when we got back upstairs and then joined the others outside. Mac showed me the graveyard, where we could glimpse the domes through the trees. We had a relaxing ride home, with Valya driving and pointing out the sights along the way. A short while later Bonnie joined us, and we were back in Sasha's car on our way to Sergeyev Posad to see Trinity Lavra, one of the largest and most beautiful monasteries in Russia. Massive white walls surrounded several 15th century churches with blue or gold domes. Vera and I stopped at some tables in the parking lot to look at traditional matryoshka nesting dolls, painted boxes, etc., while Bonnie bought souvenirs. Then we walked past several beggars near the entrance of the wall and across the stone-paved courtyard to one of the churches. Vera gave some money to a beggar standing by the door, and we stepped into another world.

My senses were immediately overwhelmed. Two small choirs were singing a-cappella, and the smell of burning candles and incense filled the air. A priest was conducting a service at the front of the church as several worshipers stood listening. Although scaffolding had been placed over a portion of the front wall, we could still see incredible painted icons surrounding large mosaic icons of Mary and the Christ Child. Frescos covered every inch of the ceiling and other surfaces. People walked in and out to light candles, and a woman walked around placing the burned-out candles into a bucket. After observing for several minutes, we walked silently past the candles for sale by the entry and continued to another church just a few yards away. We heard a male a-cappella choir and could see black-robed monks and three priests with gold mitres on their heads, but people were packed shoulder to shoulder and we could not get inside.

We passed several old (pre-revolutionary?) wooden houses as we walked from the monastery to the train station. I had been too close to the churches to capture the exquisite beauty of the domes with my camera, so while Vera went to get our tickets I bought several picture postcards at one of the souvenir stands near the station. We climbed the concrete steps to an overhead walkway to get to the other side of the tracks. The concrete was heavily worn down and the metal supports were higher than the concrete — another sign of the nation's crumbling infrastructure.

Our train to Moscow passed dachas (country homes) — new, old, some under construction, and we saw lots of people walking along the narrow paved road beside the railroad track. At the Moscow station we walked over another walkway and boarded a train going a different direction. We got off after a short ride and walked toward Vera's apartment on one of the dirt paths that appeared to randomly wander through the trees.

Vera's mother had prepared a lovely table for our celebration of Andy's baptism and Mac's birthday; Tim and Ira joined us for a deli-

Love, Vera

cious meal of meat pies, soup, cabbage pies, cake, hot tea and champagne. Vera's niece, who was visiting from Siberia, gave Mac a metal wind-up doll painted to look like a young Russian peasant girl. It had been an exciting day and was late when we walked upstairs to our apartment for a good night's sleep.

The next day we took a walking tour of Kaliningrad's main street. We passed deteriorating phone booths with missing glass and went into several shops. Each shop was stark, with nearly-empty shelves and a mixture of items, such as a motorcycle next to a few TV sets. Many people were looking, few buying. Vera advised me not to take photos but to wait until we went to Moscow, where they were used to tourists.

We stopped at an outdoor market, but Vera didn't want to wait in the long line for cabbage, so she led us to the other side of the railroad tracks. This market appeared better organized, with framed stalls and lots of people waiting in queues. Then she left me in the line for dark bread while she went to find white bread. No wonder it took so much of her time to shop — a separate queue for each item!

We carried Vera's purchases back to her apartment for a meal of fish soup and bread. After lunch we walked through the forest with Vera and Andy to buy eggs. We found Mary, the lady Vera always bought her eggs from, behind her house in a half-hector garden filled with flowers, green beans, potatoes, chickens, raspberries, etc. She greeted us warmly, offering us freshly-picked raspberries from her pail as she led us into her kitchen.

Mary (the egg lady) was delighted to have American guests in her kitchen.

As with other houses we saw in Russia, the water heater was in the kitchen, and the large kitchen windows were covered with lovely sheer lace curtains. Next to several jars of canned peaches and a bowl of fresh peaches was an appealing platter of deviled eggs, sliced tomatoes topped with a soft cheese, basil, green onions, and stuffed sweet peppers, with a few tiny flowers decorating the edge.

Mary opened a trap door in the floor and went down the ladder to her cellar to retrieve a bottle of her homemade raspberry wine. She was placing a meat jello, fried eggplant, tea, and boiled milk (chocolate) on the table just as her son Yuri came home for lunch. He had a Ph.D. in medicine and spoke excellent English, so we had an interesting visit about the many recent changes occurring in his country.

Our return walk through the peaceful forest was relaxing, and we arrived at Vera's home around 9:00 p.m. Her mother had set out meat pies and cake from the previous night and prepared a delicious salad of tomatoes and cucumbers. She and I couldn't speak each other's language, but she seemed to enjoy looking through my photo album with me after our late supper.

The next morning Vera accompanied us on the train to Moscow so we could spend time with Tamara, one of the ladies who traveled to Garden City with her son Alex the year before. Garden City's mayor, Bonnie Talley, wanted to arrange for a sister city from Russia, so Tamara had invited the Mayor of Pushkino, a small city near Moscow, to join us for dinner. Vera translated for Nikolay and Bonnie as they discussed her idea. The sister city relationship was established the following year, and Mac and I visited Pushkino when we returned to Russia in 1995.

Love, Vera

Night Train To St. Petersburg

Vera had scheduled so many wonderful things for us to see during our visit, even a trip to St. Petersburg on the night train! We were so excited when she told us about it, but I was sorry she couldn't go with us. Tamara sent her 16-year-old son Alex on the train with us as an escort and arranged for us to stay with her friends, Natasha and Alexander. Young Alex told us not to speak while boarding so no one would know we were not Russian. (Prices were higher for foreigners, and I think he bought us Russian tickets.) I have no idea what the trip cost, as our friends would not let us pay for anything during our visit to Russia. As we pulled out of Moscow, a porter delivered hot sweetened tea to us in a glass with a silver holder. Alex instructed us to lock the door and not to open it to anyone but him, and then he went into the next compartment. The following morning he told us he had slept poorly because he feared he might be robbed by one of the three other young men in his compartment.

We slept well in our comfortable roomette during the eight-hour trip. Alexander met the three of us at the train station in the morning and led us on a walking tour. I had a hard time trying to keep up with him, as he was tall and took long strides. I was glad whenever he paused in front of a few of the city's cultural gems to explain the rich history behind them.

Peter the Great founded St. Petersburg in 1703 after he was inspired by the western architecture of Amsterdam. Because of his great interest in seafaring and maritime affairs, he decided to establish a Russian port on the Baltic Sea at the mouth of the Neva River in order to trade with the rest of Europe. Thousands of peasants, convicts and prisoners-of-war were conscripted to build the numerous canals and buildings; and when the harsh climate, combined with malaria, killed tens of thousands of them, their bodies were dumped into the construction sites, leading to St. Petersburg's nickname as the "city of bones."

Peter hired European architects to design the baroque palaces and landmarks for his new city and called it his "window to the west". In 1712 he moved the capital of Russia from Moscow to St. Petersburg. His daughter, Empress Elizabeth, wanted brilliancy and luxury for Russia's court and oversaw the design of the Smolny Institute and the Winter Palace. Catherine the Great carried on the work begun by Peter and his daughter, purchasing the priceless artwork for the Winter Palace (now a part of the Hermitage Museum).

Walking toward the Savior of Spilled Blood Church in St. Petersburg.

One of the first (and most beautiful) buildings Alexander walked past was the Church of the Savior of Spilled Blood, built as a shrine to Emperor Alexander II, who was fatally wounded by political nihilists in 1881. The medieval Russian architecture, with richly decorated facade and onion domes, intentionally resembles the St. Basil's Cathedral in Moscow.

As we walked farther, Alexander explained the history of such famous places as the Smolny Convent. Built by Peter the Great for his daughter Elizabeth, it later became Russia's first boarding school for noble young ladies. Lenin proclaimed the Revolution in 1917 in this building and later set up his government there and renamed the city Leningrad.

It was a shame we didn't have time to go inside all the intriguing palaces, museums, and ornate cathedrals we passed; the beautiful exteriors and the stories Alexander told us made us wish to return for a longer visit. When he told us about the tradition of tossing a coin into the Neva River to guarantee you would visit again, Mac and I each quickly threw a coin into the water.

Alexander took us into a cozy little restaurant for lunch and made suggestions from the menu. I was ready to stop walking and was hungry, but I don't remember what I ate. Everything tasted wonderful, including the Russian champagne.

We continued walking around the city for several more hours, enjoying Alexander's fascinating descriptions. I knew almost nothing about Russian history and wished I had known before our trip that we would have a chance to visit St. Petersburg so I could have read something about the sights earlier. I'm afraid there was too much for me to absorb in our short time there.

We stopped for sundaes at a very pleasant, rather formal ice cream shop that Alexander remembered from his childhood. Each round table was covered with a cloth of teal blue, topped by a circle of glass. The rounded booths were made of inlaid wood and had teal cushions made of velvet. European ruffled sheer curtains hung over the large window behind each booth. It was definitely the nicest ice cream shop I had ever seen.

When we arrived at the apartment, we found Natasha cooking our dinner in a kitchen exactly like Vera's. She had worked all day as a computer programmer in a bank, and I imagine she had also spent time in long lines shopping for our food. She looked exhausted. Alexander had two Ph.Ds in acoustical submarines, but since jobs were scarce in Russia's current economy, he was doing post grad studies. Their two sons were spending time in the country that summer, and Natasha was renting their bedroom to us and preparing our meals to earn extra money.

On our second day in St. Petersburg, Alexander walked with us until we reached the Palace Square. Then he left us with Alex and

Love, Vera

went on to the university for the day. Alex gave us some rubles and left us in front of the Winter Palace, the main building of the Hermitage. This building was the former imperial palace of many Russian tsars and tsarinas and is now the second-largest museum in the world. We joined the other people waiting in the long queue outside the entrance. We knew no Russian, so when we finally arrived at the ticket counter, we handed our money to the lady in silence. We didn't realize we had joined the queue for Russians, and our tickets cost only the equivalent of eight cents each. Foreigners would have had to pay the enormous amount of $2.00 each to visit this world-class museum of culture and art!

As we stepped away from the ticket counter, a Russian history teacher from one of the Baltic states (Estonia maybe?) heard us speaking English and offered to show us her favorite room. She only had a short time and rushed us through numerous rooms of paintings and sculptures by world-famous artists until we reached the Malachite Room, one of the most spectacular rooms of the Winter Palace. This large salon was designed as a formal reception room for the Empress Alexandra Fyodorovna, wife of Nicholas I. It features columns, large urns, and mantelpieces of malachite mosaic set against white walls decorated with figures that represent day, night, and poetry. Virtually all the malachite used in this room was derived from Russian deposits in the Ural Mountains. Gilt doors and magnificent crimson hangings completed the room's sumptuous interior, and I remember this room as the highlight of our too-short visit to the Hermitage.

When we walked through the Egyptian collection, I paused in front of the glass case displaying a 3000-year-old mummy. As I snapped a photo of the mummy, I realized I had forgotten to disarm the flash; and the guard gave me a disapproving look. I was terribly embarrassed and left the room immediately. We had very little time to find our way back through the maze of rooms to the front entrance in time to meet Alex, so we couldn't linger as we passed by the artwork of Rembrandt, Rafael, Van Gogh, Gauguin, Pissarro, Picasso, etc. We vowed again that we would have to return to St. Petersburg another time.

Alex took us to lunch in a cafeteria located below street level. None of the other customers spoke and all eyes seemed to be watching us, making Mac and me a little nervous. The stark atmosphere was in sharp contrast to the exotic Winter Palace, and I think it was the worst meal we had in Russia. After looking over the menu, Alex suggested that the only safe food for us would be the borscht (a sweet-sour, beet-based soup with cabbage, onions, potatoes or other vegetables). We had our first taste of this soup when our Russian guests had made it for us when they visited Garden City. This cafeteria version was definitely not the same; it was thin, watery and bland. We laughed about this later, reminding ourselves that Alex had been taking good care of us and was, after all, a 16-year-old boy.

After lunch we boarded the high-speed hydrofoil to the Peterhof Palace, the ceremonial residence of Russian emperors. I'm sorry to say I didn't see the panoramic view as we crossed the waterway into the Gulf of Finland, though. Mac and I had still not adjusted to the nine-hour time difference and were so exhausted from many hours of walking in the heat that we both fell asleep soon after leaving the dock!

We woke up 30 minutes later as the boat arrived at the entrance to the Lower Park of Peterhof, sometimes referred to as the "Russian Versailles". The manicured grounds of this 247-acre estate were quite a contrast to the minimal landscaping we had seen at other attractions in St. Petersburg. French-style gardens covering a very large area included four large cascades of sparkling water, numerous gilded statues, and 150 amazing choreographed fountains, some with music. Children were playing in the flowing water of some fountains; and a few of the fountains were rigged to spray unsuspecting passers-by, an absolute delight on that hot summer day. We didn't have time to go into the enormous Baroque style Grand Palace located above the park, because Alex had one more attraction planned.

Our next stop was the restored Peter and Paul Fortress. Peter the Great had built this fortification on Hare Island in 1703 to defend St. Petersburg. It also served as a garrison and a prison for high-ranking political prisoners. The Peter and Paul Cathedral located on this island contains the tombs of all the Russian emperors. When I asked Alex where the restrooms were, he led me to a small shed behind one of the buildings and said he would guard the entrance (no door). I was a little nervous when I entered and saw that there were no lights inside, no interior doors, and no toilets. I found myself placing my feet on the painted footprints on the concrete floor and squatting over a hole in the concrete — another new experience in Russia! Alex's mom, Tamara, was appalled when she learned about it later.

St. Petersburg has over seventeen hours of daylight at the end of July, so we didn't realize how late it had become when we met a very worried Alexander waiting for us at a street corner. We bought a long-stemmed red rose for Natasha, who had prepared a delicious home-cooked meal and was waiting at the apartment. Our hosts walked Alex, Mac and me to St. Petersburg's train station after the 10:30 p.m. sunset to meet our midnight train to Moscow. I was so tired that I have absolutely no memory of reaching the train station or of our return trip. It was hard to believe how many adventures we had experienced in only seven days in Russia, and our Moscow friends had much more to show us.

TOURISTS IN MOSCOW

Vera was waiting for us the next morning to take us back to our apartment. We spent the rest of the day learning about her daily life, seeing the school where she worked as an English teacher for the primary grades, and shopping for food. When we entered a State shop, Mac spotted an abacus he wanted to buy as a souvenir of our trip. A florescent light fixture hung at an angle from the ceiling. The nearly-bare produce counter held a few small cabbages and a small pile of wilted radishes. Vera told us that the very same dented tin cans had been sitting for many months on a shelf along one wall. When I asked how she could tell what was in the identical cans with no labels, she pointed to small tags written in Russian and taped to each shelf.

Vera showing Mac unlabeled canned goods in a State shop in Kaliningrad.

In the next shop Vera gave us a lesson in shopping for meat. We waited with her in the line to choose a piece of meat and another line where she paid for her meat. Then she led us back to the meat counter to the end of the queue of people waiting to trade their receipts for their chosen meat and gave us her receipt, so we could have the experience of buying food in Russia. Next, we walked from the shop to an outdoor private market and got in line for tomatoes. As we moved from one table of produce to another, I pointed to some watermelons stacked on the ground; but she told me they were from the Chernobyl area of Ukraine and were probably radioactive. She bought food only from sellers she trusted.

Shopping for dinner took several hours, which brought back memories of her amazement at the quantity, variety, and ease of shopping for food during her visit to Garden City the previous year. On the long walk back to her apartment with our groceries, I was beginning to understand what Vera had been saying in her letters about the difficulty of her life in Russia.

One thing I didn't worry about when Barb and Mac were visiting was what to do. Moscow is a great city, and you can spend any amount of time and there will still be a lot to do and see. Besides, there are many old towns in the vicinity of Moscow with their own great history and architecture. We took them to quite a few of them, where we all enjoyed the magnificent Orthodox monasteries and churches dating back to the 12th century. It was a big contrast for people coming from such a young country as America.

We also had a lot of parties, both at home or the home of my parents, and some official ones. Everybody enjoyed themselves and communicated heartily, forgetting about the language barrier – very few people at that time knew English. There was no reason to learn English, for in the Soviet Union one had zero hope to be allowed to travel to a Western country; so why waste your time? It's different now and many people, especially the young, are encouraged to learn English. And a lot of people speak English fluently.

The following day Andy stayed home with his grandmother again, so Vera could spend the day showing us the sights of Moscow. We took the train to Komsomolskay Square, a huge open space serving Moscow's busiest railroad terminals; then Vera led us to the entrance of the Komsomolskay Metro. This station, built by forced Soviet labor, was designed by British engineers who were experienced with London's underground.

We were in for quite a surprise when we descended an extremely long escalator into what appeared to be a grand ballroom. In contrast to the aging gray block buildings we had been seeing throughout the city, a magnificent art gallery surrounded us. Stalin wanted the architecture and decor of the metro stations to be a showcase for Soviet artists and ideals, calling them "palaces for the people", so he ordered the metro's artists and architects to design structures that would encourage citizens to look up to admire the high ceilings and ornate chandeliers. Each station has a different theme, and the Komsomolskaya metro station's theme is Russia's fight for freedom and independence throughout history. High above 68 white marble Corinthian columns topped with Baroque pilasters is an imposing ceiling topped by a cupola and a spire crowned by a large star. The ceiling is decorated with eight large mosaic panels made of colored glass and precious stones. At the end of the platform is a bust of Vladamir Lenin under an arch decorated with gilt floral design and the coat of arms of the Soviet Union.

One of Stalin's "palaces for the people", the Komsomolskay Metro Station in Moscow.

Love, Vera

Of course we couldn't understand the announcements in Russian as the cars approached the stop, but I learned later that the man's voice was announcing the stops going clockwise and a woman's voice was announcing counterclockwise stops along this route.

Gypsies in Moscow. Mac told us a gypsy had pulled gently on the hairs of his forearm while we rode the train back home.

We enjoyed a relaxing afternoon seeing the sights of downtown Moscow, perusing the tables of military hats, medals, and other Russian souvenirs along the pedestrian mall on Arbat Street, and enjoying the caricaturists and music performers who were entertaining tourists. Vera stayed very close to us as we walked around downtown Moscow and cautioned us not to get too close to some of the gypsies we passed, because she thought they might steal something from us.

It was another very hot day, and Vera got excited when she noticed a young man place three cardboard boxes of ice cream on the sidewalk. She rushed over to get in the quickly-forming line, and before we finished eating our ice cream treat, the vendor was carrying away empty boxes.

Mac told me that walking onto Red Square felt surreal to him. During his service in the navy only 25 years earlier, his job had been in electronic surveillance, spying on the Russians. He was amazed that he could now walk about freely on this historic site! Now we were tourists enjoying the sights near the Kremlin — walking past Lenin's tomb — viewing ancient regalia and ceremonial objects of the 13th to 18th centuries in the Armory Museum — ogling the ornate interior and curved glass roof of GUM, the first and largest department store in Russia.

Mac and I laughed at the irony of seeing an American youth group from an evangelical church handing out leaflets to tourists by St. Basil's. They were <u>recruiting</u> in front of the cathedral that had served as the center of the Russian Orthodox church since the 16th century!

There wasn't enough time to see many of the elaborate buildings of the Kremlin, but we did go into the spectacular Kazan Cathedral to light candles. I don't have the words to express the sensation that overcame me when I walked into one of Moscow's orthodox churches, but I was overwhelmed every time I entered a sanctuary and became engulfed in the organic atmosphere of beauty, sounds, and smells inside.

Next we took the metro to an immense market in Izmailovsky Park, near the Olympic stadium. This outdoor market was a cornucopia of souvenirs, with its matryoshka dolls, samovars, antiques, etc. We each ate a tasty shish kebab that was well worth the wait in just one more long line. After Mac bought a balalaika to decorate his office and Vera helped me buy souvenirs for friends and family, we started for home.

Mac bought a balalaika while Vera and Barb shopped for souvenirs at Izmailovsky Park market.

Love, Vera

Our friend had been an excellent tour guide for us during our long day in Moscow. I wasn't used to so much walking, especially in the heat, and it was a relief to sit down during our 30-minute train ride back to Kaliningrad. I could barely stay awake while eating the delightful meal waiting for us at Vera's home, and I collapsed into bed right after walking up the stairs and into our apartment.

Our next few days were spent visiting our other Russian friends who had spent three months in Garden City the year before. First we visited Ira and Tim, where they lived with her mother and father in a Moscow apartment similar to Vera's. A table had been placed in the living room and covered with a white linen tablecloth, and we were treated to another savory Russian meal, complete with vodka toasts. I had brought my photo album of Ira and Tim's visit to Garden City, so Ira translated for her parents as they looked at the pictures.

Vera accompanied us on the train back to Moscow the next morning, so we could stay with Tamara and her husband. Unlike Vera's five-story 1960s building, Tamara's recently-built apartment building was at least 15 stories high and had elevators. One thing all apartments had in common, though, was the hot-water heating system. We happened to be visiting during the week that the water pipes in her building were undergoing an annual "flushing out". This meant that only cold water came from her faucets that week. Tamara's innovative "solution" for a hot shower was to place an electric heating element in a <u>metal</u> bucket next to the tub, which made me extremely nervous. I chose to take a cold shower at her house.

The following day Tamara took us on a fascinating tour of restored sites near Moscow. Our first stops were at two reconstructed medieval wooden churches. The Soviets had neglected or destroyed Russia's historic sites in the years since the 1917 revolution, but now the Russian people were proudly rebuilding their cultural heritage.

An unexpected delight awaited us that evening. Tamara had obtained hard-to-get tickets for the Bolshoi! I still have trouble believing we actually sat in box seats in the world-famous Bolshoi Theater and watched the Russian Ballet Company performing Spartacus. I don't know whether I was more taken with the music and those incredible dancers or the beautiful theater.

Valya was our tour guide for the next day. She arrived in a different car from the one we had seen before; and she explained to us that she needed to have two cars, so when one was broken down she could drive the other. Replacement parts were hard to get, like most things in Russia. Vera's brother Sasha had stopped one time when he saw a man standing by a parked car on the side of the road. Auto parts were spread across the hood of the car, and Sasha hoped to find a part that he needed.

Our Russian friends managed to give us memorable adventures every day. Valya chose to show us the most famous cemetery in Moscow, located outside the walls of the Novodevichy Convent. While driving us there, she explained that the Novodevichy Cemetery next to the convent had been closed to the public until the fall of the Soviet Union (only a year and a half earlier). The convent was, of course, exceptionally beautiful, but Valya seemed more anxious to show us the cemetery.

This large park-like area held the remains of thousands of famous Russian authors, musicians, poets, playwrights, scientists and political leaders. We paused by the wrought iron fence surrounding the graves of Chekhov (tall white monument) and his parents. She explained that the wall behind Chekhov's grave (a columbarium) held vaults used to store cremated ashes. Then she pointed out the sculptures and tombstones of other famous Russians, including Nikita Khrushchev and his wife.

Chekhov's grave is the tall white monument.

Valya's husband Victor was waiting at their apartment when we returned. He had a Ph.D. in mathematics, taught at the university and had published several books. He had prepared a traditional Russian meal for us of soup, cabbage rolls, a large meat loaf wrapped in cabbage leaves, tomato salad, fresh bread, black caviar, wine

Love, Vera

and, of course, vodka. Mathematicians and scientists were not permitted by the Soviets to travel to the U.S. when Victor's wife and daughter had visited Kansas the previous year, and he was eager to talk to Americans. We had all heard propaganda about each other's governments for many years, and we were curious about what life was like for the average citizen of our two countries. After a fascinating conversation over dinner, we went to see the famous Moscow circus. The performances were world class, and I learned later that tickets were not easy to get in the busy summer tourist season. Once again, our Russian friends had gone out of their way to give us a memorable experience.

Vera met us the next morning and took us to Moscow's premier foreign-art museum, the Pushkin Museum of Fine Arts. After wandering among many masterpieces of European works from ancient civilizations, the Italian Renaissance, and the Dutch Golden Age, she took us to the top of the Ostankino radio/TV tower, the tallest free-standing structure in Europe. Standing 1,772 feet tall, it was built to mark the 50th anniversary of the October Revolution. We enjoyed a leisurely lunch in the slowly rotating restaurant with a bird's-eye view of Moscow as Vera described the sights below us.

The wax museum was our next stop. When the lady in charge overheard Vera talking to us quietly in English, she scolded her for paying for tickets for Russians, rather than the slightly more expensive tickets for foreigners. As I recall, Vera was not bothered by her remarks, but I breathed easier when we left the museum and went to the Tretyakov Gallery. Several buildings held the marvelous paintings and sculptures of Russia's finest artists, and we could have spent days wandering among the impressive exhibits, rather than just a few hours. It had been another hot day filled with interesting sights and lots of walking; I was tired and happy as we boarded the train for our return to Kaliningrad.

We were nearing the end of our too-short stay in Russia, and we had not gone to Kaliningrad's city hall for the registration required of foreign visitors. Vera didn't seem concerned about it, but I worried that we would have trouble with either Russian or American authorities on our return trip home. We finally went to the city hall, only to sit in an empty waiting area for about an hour. A few people walked past us, and Vera told them something in Russian. Each one nodded and then disappeared into an office, but no one ever came out to see us. She finally got tired of waiting. She had packed a lunch for us and was anxious to go on the boat trip on the Moscow River that she had planned for that day, so we left.

We never did go back with our passports. Kaliningrad (renamed Korolev in 1996) is known as the cradle of Soviet and Russian space exploration and is home to scientists and cosmonauts in training. She told us on our last day in her town that she had just heard on her kitchen radio that foreign visitors were now being permitted to visit the city! We had no idea there had been restrictions and laughed about being American spies.

Vera had a special event planned for the last day of our visit, perhaps the best of all — a family picnic at her father's dacha. As with most older dachas near the city, the house had been divided into several small units. Her father had a bedroom and tiny kitchen on the first floor. There was an outhouse at the back of the property for all four families. Most of the land was planted with her father's very large garden, and he was fattening up two pigs for winter.

Father's house with large garden.

Vera's brother was outside getting shish kabobs ready to cook when we arrived, and his wife was in the kitchen cutting up fresh garden vegetables with Vera's

Father's tiny bedroom.

Love, Vera

mother. A table had been placed in the shade of an apple tree, and Valya was setting dishes out on the colorful tablecloth while keeping an eye on Andy and Sasha's two young sons. We spent a delightful afternoon eating, drinking father's raspberry wine, and toasting to each other in this idyllic setting. Valya and Vera translated for everyone.

The light was beginning to fade as we began our long walk back to Vera's, and everyone walked with us down the path for a while before saying goodbye. This was to be the last time we would walk through the forest. Earlier, Mac noticed that the trees were all of similar size and in straight rows, rather than scattered randomly; and he had asked about this when we were staying with Victor and Valya. Victor told him that the Germans had

Vera is in the center, feeding Andy. Mac and I are on either side of her, next to her mother and father. Her brother Sasha is behind me, and his two sons are in the front.

destroyed his country in the war, and German POWs were kept in Russia after the end of the war to repair the damage they had caused. The trees had been planted by those POWs, many of whom were not released back to Germany until Stalin died in 1953.

Our trip to Russia was certainly different from that of most tourists. We made this trip to visit our friends and had not

Vera's family walked with us as we started into the woods on the last day of our visit.

expected to see so many marvelous sights. We not only saw many of the famous tourist attractions of Moscow and St. Petersburg, but we spent time learning about the everyday lives of Vera and the other ladies who had come to Kansas the year before. We walked for hours every day, stood in line with Vera in state shops and markets, and accompanied her to buy eggs at a private home. We did not see the work our friends did behind the scenes to cook for us or stand in lines to buy tickets for the museums, art galleries, the circus, and other places they took us. In spite of the difficult economy in Russia, we were never allowed to pay for anything. We will always be indebted for their gracious hospitality.

Totally enchanted by Russia, Mac and I began planning a return trip during the flight back to the U.S. Vera had captured my heart, and our blossoming friendship has continued growing deeper for more than a quarter of a century.

I think Barb and Milton liked Russia as well as I liked America. On returning to GC they were so enthusiastic about their journey that they talked about Russia all the time. They gave talks and shared their experience with anybody who would listen. At one time I got a call from Bonnie Talley who said that Barb and Milton seemed to have gotten crazy about Russia. But so was I when I came back from America, full of stories.

Love, Vera

Politicians From Pushkino

While Mac and I were still in Russia, our mayor, Bonnie Talley, had been back in Garden City happily arranging a sister city relationship with Pushkino. We had barely had time to unpack and get readjusted to our time zone when we began preparing to host a Russian again — this time a vice-mayor from Pushkino. On September 24th of 1992 we stood on the platform of the train station with the other host families and our local Russian friend, Zina, to welcome Pushkino's mayor, three other city officials, and their female translator. We welcomed our guests with bouquets of flowers, then the travelers were each taken to their respective homes for a short rest.

After introducing my two dogs to our guest, Vice Mayor Yuri Stepchinko, I showed him around our house. Next I opened the refrigerator and pointed — my way of asking if he wanted something to eat or drink, but he shook his head. We then spent a few awkward minutes just smiling and nodding, since we could not speak each other's language. I looked at the clock and wondered what to do until he went with the others for a tour of our city's largest bank. That's when I made an embarrassing mistake. Walking over to the record player, I picked up a record and asked if he wanted to hear some music. He smiled and nodded, and as soon as the music started he took my hand and started dancing with me, holding me way too close. I realized I had given him the wrong impression and pushed him away, quickly grabbing the photo album from our recent visit to Russia and leading him to the kitchen table to show him pictures. Then I started to prepare our lunch. I was greatly relieved when it was finally time to take him to meet Bonnie for the bank tour.

Bonnie had arranged a busy schedule for the next ten days, with tours of the Iowa Beef packing plant, an agri-energy plant, a fish farm, our local zoo, city hall and city utilities, dinners at the country club and a variety of restaurants, etc. I was trying to work as much as possible on my appraisal business, but I managed to attend many dinners and events with our visitors.

We found things to enjoy in spite of our language barrier. I took Yuri to Walmart and the grocery store, and one evening the four men came to our house and played poker with Mac.

But the best day for me was when I drove Yuri and the mayor's assistant, also named Yuri, to the airport and joined them on a flight in a friend's plane — cut short, I'm afraid, because I began to get airsick.

One day Mac and I took Yuri on the two-hour drive to the McMinimy's homestead, which was established in the 1880s. While Eldora, Mac's sister-in-law, prepared her usual marvelous home-cooked meal, we visited with Mac's mom and his nieces and nephew. We had no translator, but we managed a minimum of communicating with the help of our Russian-English dictionary. Yuri smiled a lot and seemed to enjoy his day at a traditional American ranch.

On October first, their last evening in Garden City, Bonnie held a farewell picnic at her house while everyone waited for the eastbound train. We promised we would see them in Pushkino in 1994. At midnight, everyone hugged goodbye and our Pushkino visitors boarded the Amtrak train to begin their return trip to Russia.

Hand-Carried Letters

The Russian economy continued to collapse, and we sent money to Vera every time we could find someone to hand carry a letter to Moscow. Vera and Valya started to paint wooden dolls and send them to me to sell, so they could earn extra money. About a week after our visitors from Pushkino left for home, I received a package and letter from Valya, asking me to help her sell a different type of wooden doll. Each one was around two inches long, flat on the back side, and had a tiny metal loop at the top for hanging from a Christmas tree branch. Whole villages specialized in producing these dolls in the nineteenth century, and every village had its own design based on local fashion. I was to deposit the money from the sale of these dolls into the bank account she had opened while visiting Garden City.

Valya's Christmas ornament dolls, plus some new items she was trying out.

Vera's letters told of the continuing devaluation of the ruble, dropping from 150 to the dollar in August to 230-250 in September and 450 in October.

Love, Vera

This is a crazy time. If you have money, you'd better spend it fast or in two days you may have the same money but half its value. I don't make much, so I don't have to worry — it's not enough for food even. Sasha gives me the rest of what I need, so we are all right.

We are having Congress now where everybody blames the Government, but I don't see who could get the country out of this mess. In summer I hoped that we were near the bottom and as soon as we drop, we'll start climbing up. But we are still falling down — looks like it's a bottomless pit. Many people now are depressed and feel not protected and get sick. I try to 'think positive', like Bernie Siegel says in the book you sent me.

Yeltsin tried to take control of the government that fall, and in December he brokered an agreement with the Parliament to have a national referendum on a new head of government, constitution, and parliament. Vera's January and February letters talked of the holidays, the lack of postal service, and walking in the forest each day with Andy. She told me she couldn't hear me well during our last phone call because ..." *Andy broke the telephone cord with his bare hands. I mended it in haste and it didn't work well.*" (Just one more example of the poor quality of Russian goods at that time)

The increasing inflation had devalued the ruble to 650, and prices were six to seven times higher than summer.

We are all right with food, though the prices rise almost every day, but at least there is food in the shops. And I find out every time the prices go up that I can go without something else. Dollar is also subject to inflation in Russia, and I have some dollars, thanks to you, of course. I only wish they didn't ban circulation of dollars in the country. Hard times are good for our family — we get closer to each other — everybody is trying to help.

We continued to have Russian guests in our house that winter and spring and found that even though we lacked a common language, we enjoyed every experience. One night in December we hosted the mother and sister of Zina, the local Russian lady who translated for all our visitors. Their visit was a surprise Christmas gift for Zina, and it was fun to see them laughing and hugging when Zina first saw them the next day. A choir from Pushkino spent about ten days in Garden City in early 1993, and we hosted two Yuris. "Little Yuri" worked in a factory as an artist and brought a supply of watercolors to sell, so we bought all of them from him and had them framed, selling some of them after he returned to Russia. Those that didn't sell are hanging on the walls of our living room, Mac's office, and our bedroom. Later that spring we hosted two young ladies with a Russian dance group from Leningrad.

In March of 1993 the Russian parliament announced there would be no referendum after all. When Yeltsin declared he would assume certain "special powers", the parliament tried to impeach him, but they failed. So, on April 25th the Russian citizens voted on a referendum of four questions: 1) Do you trust Yeltsin? 2) Do you approve of his economic policies? 3) Is it essential to hold a pre-term election for President? 4) Is it essential to hold a pre-term election for Parliament? Vera's April letter said:

> Andy and I voted for Yeltsin (though I don't trust him) and for his economic policy, though I don't approve of it. I don't want reelections of the president, because it will be a mess, but I don't trust the Congress. So in this country I always have to say yes, when I really mean no. I just hate all politicians for making us refugees of their dangerous games.

She enclosed a charming photo of three-year-old Andy and his girlfriend standing at the edge of a lake the previous summer.

Several people from Garden City traveled to Russia in the summer of 1993, and Valya and Vera were able to send dolls home with them. I gladly took time to find a market for them to help

Andy and his girlfriend going into the lake for a swim.

my friends through very difficult times. We grew more and more concerned as Russia's political upheaval continued to worsen. Vera wrote:

> Things change so fast in this country that you will feel you are in a different place. I only hope that we'll still be here as a country. With a government like we have now we can't know what we'll have in an hour. We only survived the money exchange, and now they promise that September will be a 'hot' time. And we still don't know who's responsible for that experiment with the money exchange — the President points to the Parliament and the Parliament blames the Government. Our family didn't suffer because we didn't have any money at the moment. And we used free rides by bus and train because they wouldn't accept old notes, and small change of 1993 practically didn't exist. For tutoring Russians I get dollars and only exchange when I need rubles, since you can exchange dollars in every post office or bank or shop.

The vote for a new constitution was held in July, but the parliament wrote its own draft for a constitution. The result was dual power, with two presidents and two parliaments! Armed protesters gathered at the Russian White House (parliament building) after Yeltsin dissolved the Russian legislature on September 21st.

By October second, serious battles were occurring between troops and protesters who surrounded the TV station, resulting in an estimated 2,000 casualties. We nervously watched TV news coverage as Yeltsin ordered tanks to shell the Russian White House on the fourth of October and then arrested all members of Parliament.

Our next letter from Vera was carried out by a Christian minister on a mission and was postmarked Portsmouth, New Hampshire. She sent more dolls and a birthday gift for me and told us that many Americans had canceled their planned trips to Moscow after the events of October 4th. We were not surprised.

We continued with our plans to visit Moscow the next summer, and I began shopping for gifts to take to our friends. I also bought painting supplies for Vera's and Vayla's dolls; they had asked me to buy 16 different colors of acrylic paint, a tube of gold paint, and some fine glass paper to polish the dolls. After waiting several months to get our official invitations, we finally received them in a certified letter postmarked Tulsa, Oklahoma. About two weeks later Mac got the sad news that his older brother Bill had a brain tumor. Of course we postponed our trip. Sadly, the surgery was not successful, and Bill died six months later.

Inflation in Russia had continued soaring in 1994 as the economy collapsed. After the dissolution of the Soviet Union, the former Soviet-controlled states no longer paid taxes to Russia. Lack of resources for law enforcement brought the emergence of organized crime, and the headlines of Russian newspapers told of assassinations of business figures and shoot-outs between rival groups. The Russian government stopped paying subsidies to factories; so the child care, medical services, and housing that had been provided to workers disappeared. Factories resorted to paying their workers "in kind" (crockery, gloves, etc.), and a barter system evolved.

The dolls Vera and Valya were painting became a good source of dollars for them. Vayla brought her painted dolls to Garden City in August of 1994, and we spent three weekends going to summer festivals in southwestern Kansas to sell them. I had always loved going to our annual festival in Garden City, where a variety of interesting crafts were on display and I would see lots of my friends; but sitting at a card table in a strange town all day, smiling at strangers in the unbearable August heat, was hard work. I was glad, though, that Valya earned some money.

Vera's Oct. 26th letter was postmarked Birmingham, Alabama, Nov. 26th. She had received letters, pictures, cassettes and money from me that had taken three months to reach her. Keeping in touch was barely manageable at that time, but thank goodness people still traveled to and from Moscow.

Russian troops invaded Chechnya on December 11th, 1994, and I wondered why Vera made no mention of this in her next few letters. We watched the evening news and worried about what this might do to our country's relations with Russia, but I also avoided writing about the situation in my letters to her. She wrote about the weather, walking with Andy and recent changes that had occurred.

Love, Vera

Lots of things changed here, in fact it will be a new country when you come, a much worse country I'm afraid. It is turning into a less comfortable place to live. I went to Moscow yesterday and was depressed by what I saw — beggars everywhere, homeless kids, untidy streets, dull faces, worried faces, shops full of things most people can't afford. I can't help being worried about Andy's future.

I called Vera about once a month during the spring of 1995, and we talked mostly about Andy and our upcoming trip to Russia. I didn't tell her, but I worried that there might be another political disruption that would prevent my seeing her again. Thankfully, this didn't happen, and Mac and I were able to fly to Moscow in August.

Return To Russia — 1995

Our arrival at the Moscow airport was very similar to that of our first trip in 1992, with armed militia watching as we walked across the tarmac to the entrance and somber young men silently studying our passport photos while we slowly passed through customs. It felt so good to hug my friend after our three years apart! We talked excitedly in the back seat of the car, trying to ignore Sasha's high-speed drive on our way to Vera's apartment.

A round table with a pretty linen tablecloth stood in Vera's living room, and there was a small bouquet of red roses in the middle. She set out plates of thinly sliced salmon, artfully arranged fresh tomatoes, cucumbers and peppers (each with delicious toppings), slices of that marvelous crusty bread we had enjoyed so much on our earlier visit, and a bottle of champagne. Dessert was a cake with "Welcome" written on the top and a spoon of jam or a piece of chocolate. It felt great to be back. After dinner, Vera led us to the apartment where we would be staying during our visit. It was just a short walk from her home and had exactly the same floor plan as hers. It belonged to the parents of her friend, Olga, who were tending their garden in the country.

We spent the next day revisiting Kaliningrad. The outdoor markets in Kaliningrad appeared quite similar to those we had seen earlier, but the State shop with the dented tin cans where Mac had purchased his balalaika had become a private shop and was completely renovated, with bright colors and new light fixtures. Young ladies stood behind lighted deli cases filled with a variety of imported goods for sale at world market prices. The ladies were dressed in matching pink aprons and small pink paper hats (similar to those I wore as a teen in the 1950s when I worked in a soda fountain.).

Love, Vera

A driver in a Mercedes arrived the following morning to drive the three of us to Pushkino, Garden City's new sister city, to attend the 70-year celebration of their city. All three Yuris who had stayed in our home greeted us in the public square.

Vera translating for all three Yuris from Pushkino who had stayed with us in Garden City.

Soon I noticed that the choir members who had visited Garden City in 1993 were walking onto the stage to perform. Bonnie had given me small lapel pins to give to each of them, so I moved close to the stage, planning to give the pins to the choir members after they finished singing. I never dreamed I would be standing in front of an audience of hundreds of people when I presented those tiny pins of crossed American/Russian flags. I have no idea what I improvised in front of TV cameras and that crowd of observers; I only remember my knees shaking when someone unexpectedly guided me to the front of the stage and handed me a microphone.

After the performance, we walked with Nikolay, the mayor, to his office in Puskino's city hall. Plates of thinly sliced deli meats and cheese, fresh tomatoes, caviar-filled hard boiled eggs, carefully arranged bowls of fruit, and bottles of wine and vodka had been placed upon an extremely long table in the office. City officials and their wives began arriving. Everyone sat down together, and the officials began making toasts. About a dozen chairs at the other end of the table remained empty until a group of silver-haired men (communist city officials who had recently been voted out of office) walked in with their wives and sat down. Then the fun began. First, a retired official made a toast to communism, and everyone at his end of the table stood and cheered. A current official then toasted to "the new Russia", and everyone at our end of the table stood and cheered. The toasts continued back and forth long enough for me to begin feeling the effects of the vodka, but finally we began to eat.

As we started to leave the mayor's office, Yuri led me toward a large wall hanging of Lenin at the end of the room and pulled a chair up to the wall. Then he pulled his very tipsy American friend (me) onto a chair for a photo of all of us toasting to Lenin. That delicious peach-flavored Russian vodka sneaks up on a person.

Vice-mayor Yuri, Mayor Nikolay, Barb and Mac toasting to Lenin.

The city's celebration continued with famous professionals performing on an outdoor stage. We sat with the political dignitaries at small tables near the stage and were entertained by the music and dance of some of Russia's very best artists while drinking tea and nibbling sweet pastries and candies. The retired officials and current officials sat at different tables, of course. Pushkino's citizens stood behind a fence near us.

Vera took us to Moscow the next day and bought us all ice cream from one of the new ice cream stands near the train station.

Things had definitely changed since our previous trip, and we saw many signs of

Vera waiting for ice cream in downtown Moscow in August of 1995.

commercialization. Babushkas still swept the leaves with their straw brooms in the park outside of Red Square, but there was a line of dump trucks parked by a busy excavation site nearby. On our first visit we had wandered among the myriad of historical treasures of the Armory at no charge; now there was an admission fee and a very long line, so we didn't go inside this time.

Small kiosks stood on the wide sidewalks along Arbat Street, and newly painted signs had been placed above entrances to many old buildings. Numerous coffee shops and American fast food shops (Pizza Hut, etc.), many with outdoor seating, had replaced the vendors we had seen earlier. We bought $2.00 cups of coffee and sat down at an umbrella-covered table to people-watch for a while before returning to the train station.

Pushkino's mayor arrived with his driver the next morning to show us some of the sights of his city. He took us to see the last remaining wooden church in the Pushkino region and the grave of Father Alexander Men, a Russian priest who had been murdered in September of 1990. He was well known to Protestants, Catholics and Orthodox believers around the world for his writings and had been harassed by the KGB for his active missionary and evangelical work. Today he is still considered a martyr by many who want him to be canonized. We toured a mink and sable farm later, meeting the manager, admiring fox pelts, and trying on mink hats. Mac placed an order for hats for all three of us.

Vera returned to Kaliningrad, but the mayor's driver took Mac and me to the hotel where Vice Mayor Yuri's 50th birthday celebration was being held that evening. We entered a ballroom with sheer, floor-to-ceiling lace curtains, arches and walls carved in eloquent wooden carvings, and tables lad-

Tamara and Mac danced at Yuri's birthday party, and Barb and Yuri celebrated with vodka toasts.

en with delicacies, vodka, and enormous bottles of champagne. A live orchestra played as we ate dinner and drank many toasts to Yuri and his American guests. Mac didn't normally like to dance, but he had danced with Tamara in our living room on New Year's Eve three years earlier, and she got him to dance with her again that evening. It was truly a fun party, but I had a slight hangover the next morning after all those toasts.

Yuri and his driver took us to a lake not far from Pushkino the next afternoon. We had perfect weather to take four-year-old Andy on his first fishing trip, and he was one happy little boy when Mac helped him pull an eight-inch perch out of the water. Several people having a picnic in the nearby woods waved to Yuri as we started to drive away, so we accepted their invitation to have lunch with them. Again, we found ourselves raising glasses of vodka and champagne as everyone took turns making toasts. Then the police chief drove by and noticed our little party and decided to join us. When someone started singing Russian folk songs, the others joined in. They asked us to sing some American folk songs, but Mac and I didn't know the words to any songs from America except "The Star Spangled Banner", so we declined. Except for the cars parked within sight, it felt as though we had stepped back in time. Yuri's driver waited next to the red Mercedes until we were ready to go home. Andy, who found the car much more interesting than what was happening at the picnic table, spent the afternoon happily sitting in the driver's seat, pretending to drive.

We were in for another treat the following morning when Nikolay took us back to Pushkino to tour the factory where all the items used in Russian Orthodox churches were produced. Most churches had been closed or destroyed by the Soviets and were now being renovated or reconstructed, causing a high demand for liturgical items. An employee led us into the area where candles were mass-produced and then packaged by hand. More than sixty ladies sat at sewing machines in another area of the factory busy making robes for priests. Other women were running an enormous embroidery machine, sewing designs of gold thread onto a long white runner to be used for a communion table. One spacious room had more than twenty artists

Love, Vera

painting icons with egg tempera paint and gold leaf or painting outdoor scenes of Russia in watercolor. We saw Little Yuri and stopped to talk with him for a few minutes. Our tour ended in a show room displaying ornate liturgical items used in an Orthodox church, such as gilt candlesticks, light fixtures, crosses, and altar tables inlaid with gold leaf.

Showroom in the Pushkino factory where liturgical items were produced for the Russian Orthodox Churches.

Before we returned to Pushkino, Nikolay took us back to the mink factory to pay for the hats we had ordered earlier. We noticed factory workers trying to sell mink hats along the side of the road as we drove away; they had obviously been paid with hats instead of money.

Yuri took us to spend that afternoon with his friend, the owner of a construction firm. He was wealthy enough to have purchased land and built a new dacha, which he was quite proud of. His wife served us a vegetarian lunch, and then he wanted his guests to try his new sauna. When it was Vera's and my turn, she showed me how I should gently slap birch branches against my skin to stimulate the blood flow. She seemed to love the experience in the suffocating heat, but I only felt extremely hot, silently wishing to get out of the sauna as soon as possible. Our hostess served everyone watermelon, wrapped candies, and hot tea outside on the patio before Yuri took us back to Vera's.

Because he was a politician, Yuri was also able to buy a plot of land and build his own dacha. We went there the next day with Tamara as our translator. Yuri's three sisters from other towns were visiting for a few days and helped their mother prepare lunch while Yuri showed us around his house and enormous garden. His piece of land was large enough for his story-and-a-half dacha plus the garden, a greenhouse, and a covered picnic shelter with several tables, in addition to his father-in-law's rabbit house about the size of a single-car garage.

When Yuri had stayed at our house three years earlier, I told him I wanted him to feel at home and showed him how to run the dishwasher. He seemed surprised that Mac washed our dishes, telling me that men did not do this in Russia. Now we were visiting his house, and he laughed while telling Mac and me he wanted us to feel at home, so we needed to do some chores. He gleefully showed Mac how to cut wood with his electric saw and told me to wash the samovar in the tub of cold water outside by the garden.

Yuri's father-in-law invited us into the rabbit house and proudly showed us several dozen cages filled with rabbits. I had never eaten rabbit before and didn't realize I would soon be making myself choke down a few bites of one of those cute little bunnies. Those vodka and champagne toasts probably helped. We spent the afternoon picking a few mushrooms in the woods behind the dacha and then swimming in a lake just a short walk away. When we got out of the water, we learned we had been swimming in the reservoir that was the water supply for Moscow — no swimming allowed! I was mortified, but Yuri thought it was funny. His son was cooking shish kabobs when we arrived back at the dacha, so we ate <u>again</u>. His sisters kept Tamara busy translating their countless questions about America until it was time for us to leave.

It seemed the men from Pushkino never ran out of ideas for adventures for their American friends. The next morning we went on a pilgrimage to a holy spring about an hour's drive northeast of Moscow. We traveled in a caravan of three cars with Tamara, Yuri's sisters, and a neighbor and his son. Eventually we left the paved highway and bumped along a dirt road filled with deep ruts, parking when we reached a dirt path that disappeared into the forest. Because that day was a special holiday in the Orthodox church, a priest was standing near a sign posted at the beginning of the path and praying with people as they arrived.

We climbed to the top of some long wooden steps and saw several women watching a group of men getting in and out of a pool of water. The men in our group stripped to their bathing suits and stepped into the pool. After the men finished bathing, we women removed the clothing over our bathing suits and stepped in and out of the shockingly cold water — three times.

Love, Vera

Men bathing in the icy water of the holy spring.

    Yuri's neighbor had brought a ten-gallon metal milk can and filled it with holy water that had been blessed by the priest, and Mac helped him carry it back to his car. We took a small jar of that water home to give to Donna Skinner, who had hosted Tamara when she visited Garden City. Donna had recently discovered she had a rare form of blood cancer, and we kidded her after she recovered that the holy water had been the reason for her recovery. We ended our day's adventure with lunch in a restaurant, where Yuri ordered "some of everything" for us and his family. We even had both red and black caviar with our meal.

    Vera, Mac and I were all quite fond of Little Yuri (as we called him in order to distinguish him from the other two Yuri's who had stayed at our house), so we took the train to Pushkino the next day and met him just outside the city at his dacha. The old wooden house had been divided into several small units, similar to the dacha where Vera's Father lived. Little Yuri wanted to show us his garden behind the house. There was also a greenhouse and a small shed where he raised chickens. We bought some roses for his wife before going to their apartment. She had worked for 26 years to earn the right to buy this new apartment upon her retirement. It was decorated with Yuri's framed paintings on the walls and lovely sheer lace curtains over the patio doors. We enjoyed a leisurely lunch with Yuri, his son, his wife and her niece, who also lived with them.

Our next day began with Sasha driving the three of us to see the Botik Museum, about an hour from Vera's home. One of the first wooden sailing ships of the Russian navy, which had been started by Peter the Great in 1698, was on display along with other naval relics from that time. A corner of the building had recently been remodeled into a restaurant, and Sasha bought us all pizza. On the way home, we stopped at a small wooden chapel next to the road that had been used by Peter when he had traveled in this area the late 1600s.

We rode the train to Moscow the next afternoon to spend the night with Valya and Victor. Valya, ever the entrepreneur, took us the next morning to see her newest business — providing custom-designed ceiling tiles for apartments in old buildings that were being remodeled. She hired unemployed engineers who could not find white-collar work in the current economy to design and install the ceiling tiles. The business eventually became so profitable that the mafia moved in and demanded protection money from her, so she had to close it the next year. After having lunch with Ira (another visitor to Garden City), we spent several hours gazing at the magnificent art on display at the newly remodeled Tretyakov Gallery of Russian Art.

Each day of this second trip to Russia had been filled with interesting, fun adventures, but our next two days were the best. We were lucky enough to be visiting on September 1st, the first day of the new school year. I had no idea what a delightful tradition we were about to observe as we walked with Vera to the building where she taught English to primary level students.

Parents and students were waiting near the front steps when we arrived. The

On the first day of school, September 1st, Vera took us into one of the classrooms where she taught English.

older students wore navy skirts and white blouses or navy slacks and white shirts. Little girls were wearing navy blue dresses with white lace collars, white tights, and pretty shoes. Each girl had a large white organdy bow on her head. The young boys wore navy blue suits and neckties. The principal welcomed the crowd of people gathered by the steps, and then a group of students sang a song.

Next, an eleventh-grade student lifted a first-grade girl to his shoulders and walked with her up the steps while she rang a brass hand bell to announce the official opening of the school year. Then each of the other eleventh-grade students took the hand of a first grader and walked with him or her through the entrance and to his or her classroom. Vera told us that on the last day of school, the first graders walk the graduating eleventh grade students out of their school. (Russian schools consist of eleven grades.)

Vera, Mac, and Andy on our boat ride on the Moscow River.

That afternoon we took the train and metro to Moscow for Andy's very first boat ride. After enjoying the delicious picnic lunch Vera had brought along, we went up on deck to gaze for the last time at Russia's capital city and the Kremlin. Vera seemed to get immense pleasure from our relaxing afternoon cruise on the Moscow River. Andy had bonded with Mac, staying close to him all day and sitting on his lap during the return train ride back to Kaliningrad.

One more special event was planned for us — a picnic at her father's house with Vera's extended family the following day. Sasha, his wife, and her sister were cooking shish kabobs near the edge of the garden when we arrived. Vera's mother and a friend were placing platters of fresh fruit and garden vegetables on the table, which also held a nine-layered cake dripping with frosting and another cake topped with frosting and raspberries. Vera's father brought out a tray with glasses and a bottle of vodka and set it next to his homemade wine on another table.

We spent a delightful afternoon under the shade of the apple tree sharing wonderful food and wine and, of course, making vodka toasts to each other. Little Yuri arrived in time for dessert and presented a beautiful framed painting to Vera's mother. After joining us for several more toasts, he and Vera's father began singing Russian folk songs

Little Yuri, Vera's father and mother, and Mac at the family picnic.

for us. What fun! Andy spent the afternoon at his favorite pastime, sitting with his cousin in his Uncle Sasha's car.

I felt terribly sad saying goodbye to everyone as we began our walk back through the forest. Vera's mother walked a short way with us, and I couldn't hold back tears as we hugged each other goodbye. Somehow I knew I would never see her again.

Our last day in Russia was a sad day of packing and saying goodbye to Vera and Andy. Nikolay came from Pushkino and Valya came from Moscow for a goodbye dinner at Vera's home that evening. We toasted to our friend from Pushkino and invited him to visit us again. We also invited Valya and Vera to come back to our house.

Love, Vera

Letters And Phone Calls

Letters and phone calls between Vera and me continued over the next several years. We talked often of the wonderful memories of our previous visits together and our hopeful plans to see each other again. Vera continued teaching at an elementary school during the weekdays and tutoring evenings. She had told me her dream was to save enough money to have her own country house with enough land for a large garden. In June of 1996 she wrote about finally buying that house.

At last I bought a house. I helped the assessor measure the house and draw the floor plan required by the government when a house is sold, and I thought about you, Barb, and remembered how I once went with you to measure a house in Garden City. It wasn't a very good house, I remember, but my house is much worse. It has one small room, a kitchen (half of which is a wood-burning stove) and a covered entrance. But I think it's more than enough for Andy and me. The house needs a lot of repairing, but I can't do everything in one summer. I hired a man to repair the floor. It seems more important now because I don't want holes in the floor — rats might come to the room. Next summer I will have

Back view of Vera's house in the country before repairs were made.

to replace the window frames — the wood is so old that you can't open the window — it can go to pieces.

There is a garden near it, too. And it's rather large — larger than Father's. I planted some vegetables and potatoes. (I used the seeds you brought me, too.) The land is very hard; it was quite a job to dig it — I couldn't stand up right afterwards. Now I'm anxious to see what will grow. I don't expect much, of course, but there are bushes of currents and raspberries, gooseberries and plums. And there are also some apple trees and cherries. I hope I'll have quite a harvest.

Vera ready to tackle the weeds in her future garden.

Every summer Vera worked long hours in her garden, carrying water from a nearby well and using hand tools to clear away weeds and brush. Each year she canned fruits and vegetables and made jams and jellies to take back to their apartment for the winter. I asked Vera to tell me about the village where she spent her summers, and she wrote back with the following:

Barb, you asked what a village is. A village in Russia is a small settlement away from the city where people are agricultural workers. There are two or three streets, sometimes one with small houses. Every family has a house of their own. The houses are small — all of them have a kitchen and one room which is a bedroom and a living room at the same time. (Even if there are six or more people in the family, they all sleep in it.) There is also a small room that can only be used in summer. There are two stoves in the house to heat the room and the kitchen. (We have one in the wall between the room and the kitchen, because we don't live here in winter.) The house is connected with a barn and a shed, where they keep tools and animals. The wages here are so low that it is only enough to buy salt, matches and bread. (I get about 300 dollars — and that is far from enough, but here they get between 10 and 50! Those who earn 50 are called "the rich"!) So every family has a cow or two, several pigs, hens, some have goats, sheep or geese. But in spite of growing so much meat, they hardly ever eat it. They sell meat, eggs, potatoes, leaving very little for themselves. The whole village forms a kind of cooperative; they work in the field or on the farms and get wages, doing their work in the garden and taking care of their animals in their free time. So women get up at 4 a.m. to milk the cow and sometimes can only go to bed at 11. Most men drink vodka, and some women do, too. They produce food and sell it at very low prices, and in the cities we buy it at high prices. The people who are in between get very rich. For example, they buy milk from the farms at a price of 2.50 and sell it to us for 12 rubles or more.

We "summer people" are very welcome there — we buy milk for 3.50 — and we also save money. So, as a rule, people here are very friendly, and I enjoy life here. Andy goes free — I don't have to follow him, and it's so quiet here that I can hear his voice most of the time. And he is quite wild — he doesn't want to read, and I don't know if he will write to you. The same kids come to stay for summer, and when they first meet they are so happy that we can't make them stay at home for a minute — they come to eat and to sleep. Andy helps me carry water from the well. I have a lot of work in the garden, but it can wait. I don't expect a big harvest. The busiest times will come in two or three weeks, when I will be making jam and canning pickles. Anyway, it's better here than at home, and I hope the weather is good.

Love, Vera

Her next letter was written in October of 1996.

> Mother has been very busy making stores for winter — we had a very good harvest in two gardens. Father helps her. Sasha works hard and sometimes goes hunting or fishing — without success, though. Summer was very busy: in fact, it was so busy that I didn't have time to enjoy my new house in full. The garden is very big, and it was in a bad state — I had to cut many trees and to weed and water the garden. Andy was very happy. He was quite free there — I didn't have time to look after him properly.
>
> I work even more than last year — I will need a lot of money to repair the house. Andy is now staying with mother and father three days every week. He hates day care, and I try to make it easier for him. His teachers say I spoil him, that he must do what every child of his age does, but I think I must do everything I can when I can still do it for him. Who knows what is in store for him in the future? I'm getting very worried about what is happening in this country.

We talked on the phone several times over the next year. Her letters were now coming with a postmark from Moscow and began arriving within two weeks, though I still relied on finding someone to hand-carry most of my letters so we could send money with them. We eagerly looked forward to hearing about Andy and getting photos that were sometimes included. He started school in September of 1997.

> In the whole, I'm pleased with the way Andy studies — he is serious and always does his homework. His favorite subject (apart from P.E.) is English and he also likes computer lessons. (They have them once a week.) He also likes music and says he is going to be an architect and a jazzman. He is a Taurus and likes beautiful things, and he dreams about building palaces and castles. Children nowadays draw heroes like Batman or Spiderman, but Andy draws nice country houses surrounded by beautiful gardens.

Yeltsin continued making radical economic reforms, including price liberalization, mass privatization, and stabilization of the ruble.

Despite these reforms, the economy performed horribly throughout the 1990s. Numerous bouts of inflation decimated the savings of Russian citizens, and their disposable incomes rapidly declined. Oil prices dropped at the end of 1997, and by the middle of 1998 Russia devalued the ruble, defaulted on its debt, and declared a moratorium on payments to foreign creditors.

Zina took her daughters to visit her family in Minsk in May of 1998. She saw Vera in Moscow and brought us her next letter. Vera and Andy were planning to see us in Garden City that summer.

When I left you, I was sure (deep in my heart) that I'd never see you again. (Remember what country it was — the USSR.) I thought it was a miracle that we escaped from there for a while and then the iron curtain would separate us forever. And now being so far from each other we still have connections, even through our friends, and we can share news.

Andy is very excited about our visit to you, and I am, too. I'm taking him to meet Zina's daughters tomorrow, because I want him to hear for himself that they speak English. He believes, or rather knows, that Americans speak English, but when I said that American kids also speak English he didn't believe me. (Are you kidding? How could they learn?) So tomorrow he will see for himself.

On June 8, 1998, Vera wrote that the waiting list for passports was 500 people, with two employees — no hope for their passports before September. She asked if the end of May or early June of 1999 would be O.K. for Mac and me.

Andy and I are both excited. He is still undecided about having to fly and hopes we can work out some other way of getting to you. (Suppose they build a tunnel under the Atlantic Ocean by that time? Let's go to South America somehow and then we'll only have to cross the Panama Canal.) When I dismiss all his suggestions, he says, "OK, we'll have to take a risk." But I'm sure it will be no problem because he really wants to go.

Her letter written on October 11, 1998, said:

They accepted my application for the passport. To be able to give them my papers, I had to come to Moscow three times a

Love, Vera

week to "check the lists". I had been doing that for more than a month, collecting all the necessary papers meanwhile. I'm glad I'm through with it and now, if everything goes well, I'll have the passport in one and a half months. Andy studies the globe and knows now there is no other way to get to America than by air and says, "OK, so we'll have to take a risk." I hope the situation in Russia doesn't change dramatically by the time we come in May. It's not clear at the moment what's going on — prices went up 200-300% and salaries are the same.

We talked by phone in January of 1999, and Vera asked me to send a letter inviting them for a May or June visit. It was apparently still required for the officials in Moscow before she could travel. They finally arrived in Garden City in the summer.

ANDY TAKES A RISK

I came back to GC in 1999. This time I was with my son, who by that time was able to speak and understand English. I only agreed to come when Barb and Milton assured me that a limited group of friends would be informed of my stay, and I wouldn't have to give talks twice a day. I did it once and enjoyed meeting people who were genuinely interested in my country. This time I wanted a quiet stay so that I would be able to enjoy my friends' company to the full. It was a hot, dry Kansas summer. Barb took a vacation and we both enjoyed our free time together. For me it was a real break from hard, everyday work and many worries — life in Russia in the '90s was very difficult. We spent our time mostly talking and occasionally meeting our friends.

Barb and Milton had a very special gift for their godson — a trip to visit her mother in Florida and to see Disney World. Although Andy says he doesn't remember much of the trip (especially when he was naughty), I have a very clear memory of it. I enjoyed every minute, and Milton and I took all the most frightening rides and even did some of them twice. Barb and Andy didn't seem to be willing to take a risk, and Barb was kind to stay with Andy, letting me be a child for a while. Thank you, Barb and Milton.

What an adventure it was, taking eight-year-old Andy to Disney World! Mac and I still laugh at the memory of taking him to his first 3-D movie (possibly his first movie ever). He was startled when the air vent below his seat made something brush against his ankles, and he kept his feet up on the chair after that. He managed to keep watching the movie a while longer — until the snake slithered from the screen toward his face! Andy was out of that seat and heading for the exit in a flash, and we all had to scramble to keep up with him!

Love, Vera

    Visiting a farm was another pleasurable activity. I was curious about rural life in America, and we had a great chance to get to know more about it. And staying in the company of Sam and Nancy Douglas was a very special experience, of course. Andy was fascinated with the machinery and Sam even let him drive some. Sam and Nancy have a big family and knew very well how to deal with children, so Andy was nice all the time. Thank you, Sam and Nancy.

    Nancy took us to the local museum. It was great! America is a young country, but people keep the artifacts from their past with loving care and scenes from the old times are seen vividly. We also went to church and visited the fields where huge combine harvesters were working. We enjoyed talking with the combine driver. It was a very clever thing, the way they started harvesting in the South of the country and then gradually moved to the North as the wheat got ripe. Thus, they had work all summer.

    Another thing that was quite different from Russia was that the farm was located separately, with no other people around. In Russia farmers lived in villages where there would be at least one street of houses. And all the machinery would be in collective use. Each family would have a cow or two, some pigs, hens, and so on. They would grow all possible kinds of vegetables, and I was especially surprised when Nancy went to the supermarket and bought vegetables there. But perhaps the biggest surprise was Nancy herself — too refined and delicate to be a farmer or even a farmer's wife.

Enduring Friendship

Vera and I continued our long-distance friendship through letters, phone calls, and eventually emails during the next several years. She wrote about Andy's progress in school and their summers in the village. She continued tutoring several hours a day to earn money for improvements to their dacha. Andy worked on that old house every summer and eventually remodeled it completely. It's hard to believe it is the same house Vera bought in 1996!

Exterior and kitchen of their country house after Andy remodeled it.

Love, Vera

Mac and I retired in 2006 and moved to the beautiful state of Oregon. Vera and Andy visited us in 2011, the year before Andy graduated with an architectural degree in interior design.

We live only an hour from the Coast, and it was fun showing them this beautiful part of America. We took them on a whale watching trip in Depot Bay and showed them our favorite spots in Newport. Then we met Donna Skinner in Yachats and spent two nights at a small motel at the edge of the ocean where we could listen to the crashing waves from our rooms.

Twenty-year-old Andy with Mac in Eugene, Oregon, in the summer of 2011.

Staying with your friends and enjoying their warm welcome makes such sweet memories! Our friends Barb and Milton hosted us the longest, and it seems to be a miracle that they never showed their annoyance, although I know very well what a nuisance I can be. They live in Oregon now, and I've visited them twice there. It's a fabulous place. We went to see Crater Lake and Yellowstone and enjoyed staying by the ocean several times. All those places are wonderful, but visiting with Barb and Milton made them really special.

I was very happy when I learned that Donna Skinner was going to join us in Yachats. We spent two days remembering the wonderful times we had in Garden City and Moscow. Donna is full of stories, and Barb and I took advantage of every waking minute with her.

I still marvel at the fact that 28 years ago Vera came into my life as a complete stranger from the other side of the world and has become one of my dearest friends. We no longer have to wait weeks for a letter but can visit on Skype regularly. Internet and cell service recently became available in her village, so we can even communicate in the summers now. We live on opposite sides of the earth, eleven time zones apart, but we are never far away from each other in our thoughts. Writing about our years of friendship has brought back so many wonderful memories, and I hope she will come to Oregon one more time so we can sit together on the patio with a glass of wine and reminisce.

Recently, Barb wrote that I had dropped in on them from out of the blue sky. I am so grateful to God I did it! Looking back at this long-time friendship, I realize that it was a miraculous experience I've had making friends with people of a different culture and finding so many things that we have in common. We have different backgrounds, different family lives, almost opposite political views, and still we have managed to stay friends. And I feel that we are not just friends, we are family. When I write at the end of my letters, "Love, Vera", I really mean it.

Love, Vera

Love, Vera

About The Authors

Vera Penkova was born in 1955 in Omsk, Siberia. After graduating from Omskiy State Pedagogical University with a degree in English and German languages, she moved to the Moscow suburban city of Kaliningrad (renamed Korolev in 1996). She recently retired from teaching English classes for primary and high school students in the Korolev schools and continues tutoring English in her home. Vera visited Barb and Milton McMinimy twice in Kansas and twice in Oregon during the past 28 years and hopes to make another visit in the near future.

Barb McMinimy graduated from Kansas State University with a bachelor's degree in music education and a master's degree in school administration and elementary education. After working in school administration for several years in the Kansas City area, she moved to southwestern Kansas with her husband and obtained a designation as a Senior Residential Appraiser (SRA). She had her own real estate appraisal business when the five Russian ladies arrived in Garden City, Kansas, in 1990. She served on several city advisory committees and volunteered for local non-profits, such as the Sister Cities Committee; and she and her husband enjoyed hosting many international visitors. They traveled to Moscow in the summers of 1992 and 1995 to visit Vera and several Russian officials from the Moscow region who had been guests in their home. She retired in 2005 and is living in Eugene, Oregon, with her husband Milton (Mac) and their Cocker Spaniel, Sita.

Love, Vera

ADDENDA

City of Travelers Rest

160 State Park Road
Travelers Rest, SC 29690

March 16, 1990

Dear Ladies:

We received your letter at our town on March 12th. It was forwarded to us at Travelers Rest, South Carolina by the Postmaster of Tigerville, South Carolina. Tigerville is a very small village that doesn't have an organized government, therefore they have no mayor.

The people of our town and surrounding area will be very pleased if you can visit us. We are a small town at the foothills of the mountains and are quite proud of our neighborhood.

We are in the process of making the necessary arrangements and hope that these arrangements will be completed in the very near future. We would like to know approximately when you would like to visit, how long you would like to stay and how many people would like to come.

Please write us as soon as possible so that we can complete the arrangements. If there is a telephone number and a time we may call you, please let us know. We are looking forward to meeting each of you in person in the very near future.

Yours very truly,

C. Murray Garrett
Mayor

CMG:km

Gateway To The Blue Ridge

Love, Vera

Giles County
Chamber of Commerce

Municipal Building
Pulaski, Tennessee 38478
Phone (615) 363-3789

BETTIE HIGGINS
EXECUTIVE DIRECTOR
SARAH MARGARET SMITH
ASSOCIATE DIRECTOR

BOARD OF DIRECTORS
John Murrey, President
Bill Jobert, Vice-President
Dr. John Mann, Secretary-Treasurer
Dot Cheatham
Kaye Edwards
Steve Garrett
Chuck Hill
Melinda Hughey
Billy Kennedy
Hershel Lake
William A. McNairy
Phil Wilson
Beth Holley, Ex-Officio
Mayor Dan Speer, Ex-Officio
County Executive Officer Earl Wakefield, Ex-Officio

March 28, 1990

Dear Russian friends,

We hope you have received our package of information. We are eager to hear from you again.

Since you wrote to us, we have had a lot of our citizens say they are very interested in the possibility of your coming to Pulaski to visit for several months. We have had one job offer and a very good possibility for housing for you.

Since rubles are not traded on the world market and cannot be exchanged for other currency, I do not know exactly how that situation will work. However, I am confident something can be worked out. The nearest large city to us is Nashville, Tennessee (which is the capital city of our state). Planes fly into there regularly from New York which is probably where the Soviet Aeroflot would land. What I don't know is how you would purchase a ticket to Nashville - perhaps there is some type of arrangement between Aeroflot and an American airline company that would enable you to purchase tickets all the way to Nashville rather than just to New York. There are at least a dozen American airlines. Most of them fly into Nashville. We would meet you in Nashville and drive to Pulaski.

As you think about coming if you need a specific invitation or something of that sort please let us know by letter. Please also let us know if there is anything we need to do from this end toward helping get visas, etc.

We have followed, with great interest, the news from the Soviet Union. These are not easy days for your citizens nor your leaders. We hope for the very best and that people everywhere will be able to live in peace and freedom.

Sincerely,

Bettie Higgins

Chanute and Garden City may share Soviet visitors

Both cities receive letters

By JANE NEUFELD
Staff Writer

Garden City and Chanute received identical letters from four Soviet women interested in visiting, Garden City Mayor Bonnie Talley said.

"We're talking in terms of kind of sharing them," she said.

The two cities have discussed an arrangement in which the women would spend three months here and three months in Chanute, she said.

The Soviet women wrote that the Iron Curtain seemed to be lifting now, and for the first time in their lives they saw an opportunity to travel to the West.

They said they were interested in living and working for several months in an American small town or on a farm. Two of the women had children, and would like them to attend school here during the visit.

Talley doesn't know whether other towns in Kansas besides Garden City and Chanute have received the letter, although she suspects the women might have written to a number of towns to improve their prospects of a favorable response.

But Garden City already has started the ball rolling to try to bring the women here.

City officials have contacted U.S. Sen. Nancy Kassebaum's office to obtain the forms necessary to arrange a visit. Talley has written back to the women, although she has not yet received a reply from them. She is hoping to have one soon.

Before forms for the visit can be filled out, some more information about the women is needed, Talley said. For example, the letter listed only the years of their births and their exact dates of birth are needed.

Talley said she'd received calls or letters from numerous people about the visit. She said a Nebraska farmer called and offered to house the women, apparently thinking there wouldn't be enough Garden Citians interested in housing them.

The opposite is true, she said. She's been flooded with offers from people interested in opening their homes to the women.

"People are really interested in this right now. It seems to be rather timely," she said.

She admits she's worried that tensions between the Soviet government and the Baltic republic of Lithuania might spoil the chances for a visit. Lithuania is trying to break free of the Soviet Union.

Talley said the conflict could cause the Soviet Union to withdraw some of the new freedoms it has offered.

The women live near Moscow, Talley said. One of them wrote that she was an English teacher and the letter was written in English, although the envelope contained writing in Cyrillic, the Soviet alphabet.

Talley said she wrote back in English and tried to write the address in Cyrillic just as the women had written it.

The women's letter arrived at city hall here in mid-February. That's about the same time a letter arrived in Chanute, said Robert Walker, Chanute city manager.

He said Chanute had not extended an invitation for the women to visit, but had contacted its Congressman to check on the possibility of a visit.

He found out Garden City had received a letter through a newspaper article about it. He has spoken with Talley, and Chanute is interested in sharing the women's visit if it can be arranged.

Walker said it would give the women a perspective on two different Kansas towns in two different parts of the state. Chanute is in southeast Kansas.

"It would just widen their experiences while they're here," he said.

Like Talley, he did not know whether other towns had received letters but suspected some might have.

The women signed their names to the letters in Cyrillic. The translations, as provided with the help of the Adult Learning Center, are:

Valentina Constantinovna Zharinova, programmer, born in 1944; daughter Maria, born in 1977

Valentina Vladimirovna Chirka, medical-biologist, born in 1945

Tamara Ivanovna Soboleva, physics teacher, born in 1945; son Alexei Osipov, born in 1976

Vera Vladimirovna Penkova, English teacher, born in 1955.

Love, Vera

TOWN CLERK
JEAN T. BARKER

TOWN MANAGER
DANA J. REED

MUNICIPAL OFFICES
93 Cottage Street
Bar Harbor, Maine
04609-0337
207-288-4098

April 18, 1990

Dear Ladies:

I was very pleased to receive your letter regarding visiting the United States to learn more about our traditions and way of life. As you noted in your letter, this is a very interesting period in our lives as our two countries work to establish friendly relations. I would hope that we could do our part by arranging a visit for you to the United States this summer or fall.

Bar Harbor is a tourist community. Our winter time population of 4124 grows to nearly 24,000 in the summertime, as an estimated four million people per year visit Acadia National Park. I have included an advertising pamphlet put out by the Bar Harbor Chamber of Commerce, which should give you some idea of the community in which we live.

Should you be interested in coming here to live for a few months, I am fairly confident that we could locate housing and temporary jobs in the tourism industry, at the Jackson Laboratory or at the High School.

In order to extend an official invitation from the Town of Bar Harbor I must speak with my governing body, the Bar Harbor Town Council. Should they be interested in extending an official invitation I will be getting back with you at that time.

Thank you for writing to the Town of Bar Harbor. I apologize for the length of time it has taken me to respond to your letter. However, this is a very busy time of year for me. I shall look forward to hearing from you.

Sincerely yours,

DANA J. REED
Town Manager

DJR:jtb
Encl.

Russian visitors to arrive Friday

Finally, Garden Citians have their first opportunity to meet our Russian friends who are going to be arriving in international Garden City at 8:05 a.m. Friday on Amtrak. Valentina K., Irinia, Tamara, Valentia V. and Vera — along with Valentina K.'s daughter Maria, Tamara's son Alexsi and Irinia's son Artem — will be happy to meet all of you.

We are planning a big welcome at the Amtrak station complete with flags representing the nationalities of Garden Citians, signs, balloons and flowers. There will be coffee and doughnuts and we want as many of you to come as possible. There will also be Russian and American national anthems.

If you can't come on Friday morning, please bring a covered dish and your own table service (plate, glass, fork, etc.) and join us at the Community Church (across from the library) at 7 p.m. Saturday.

If you can't make either of these, please join us at the Wheat Lands Convention Center at 6:30 p.m. Tuesday for our Annual Sister Cities Banquet. Just call the Wheat Lands to make your own reservations as early as possible.

They will be scheduled to speak at most of the service clubs in the three months they will be here. If you have any events you want to share with them, please call Emily Barkley at 276-1168, Milt McMinnimy at 276-4028, Gene Skinner at 275-7521 or Bonnie Talley at 276-2675. We want to give them a good old Garden City international welcome.

BONNIE TALLEY
1507 Willow Lane

Love, Vera

Soviet travelers are headed for Garden City

Nothing went wrong at the last minute and a group of Soviet women finally is in the United States, headed for Garden City.

City Commissioner Bonnie Talley said the five women and their three teenage children arrived yesterday in Washington, D.C. They were to board Amtrak today and head to western Kansas, with a layover in Chicago.

The public is invited to greet them when they arrive here. The train is scheduled to arrive at 8:05 a.m. Friday. A welcoming ceremony is planned.

The women first wrote to "Mr. Mayor" of Garden City in February. They wrote that the Iron Curtain was lifting and they wanted to visit a rural community or small town in the United States to see what life is like in the West.

Talley, who was then Garden City's mayor, began the long bureaucratic process of arranging a visit. The Sister Cities Committee has been coordinating the visit.

The women will spend three months here and three months in Chanute, to which they also wrote. They will stay with host families.

Talley said they speak English, although some are more proficient than others. They plan to speak to a number of service clubs while here.

Service clubs and individuals donated more than $1,000 in a week to help pay for the group's train tickets.

The Garden City Telegram

— The Editor's Opinion —

Soviet visitors

The Russians are coming! And we're glad they are.

Garden City will roll out the red carpet tomorrow morning when a group of eight Soviet visitors arrives on the westbound Amtrak train.

The group — which includes five women and three teenagers — wrote several rural communities last February. They said they were interested in visiting a rural community in the United States to see what life is like in the West.

Residents in Garden City and Chanute responded to the letters and helped arrange a visit. The visitors will spend three months here and then move to Chanute for another three months.

Locally, Bonnie Talley, city commissioner, and the Sister Cities Committee have helped make all the arrangements.

Now the rest of us can join in and make the Soviets' stay in our town a wonderful experience.

There will be a welcome ceremony when the train arrives tomorrow morning at the Amtrak station on South 7th Street. Scheduled arrival time is 8:05 a.m.

There will be other chances to meet the Soviet visitors. There will be a covered dish supper at 7 p.m. Saturday at the Community Church, 710 N. 3rd. That will be followed in a few days by the Sister Cities Committee's annual banquet at 6:30 p.m. Tuesday at the Wheat Lands Convention Center.

Join in the activities. Show our visitors from the Soviet Union that we're glad they're here.

Love, Vera

WELCOME — Garden City's Vice-mayor Dennis Mesa welcomes Russian visitors with gifts at the Amtrak station this morning.

Cheers greet Soviet visitors

'Best of friends' meet following year of letters

By JANE NEUFELD
Staff Writer

A crowd broke into cheers and applause this morning as the first of five Soviet women stepped off the train at Garden City.

"Are you Bonnie Talley? For a year we've been the best of friends," Tamara Ivanovna Soboleva said as she set foot in Garden City.

It was Bonnie Talley. And it was, finally, in person, a group of Soviet visitors standing in Garden City.

About 60 people greeted the five Soviet women and their three teenage children with balloons, flowers, flags, welcoming signs and applause.

"On behalf of our small group, I want to thank you for a terrifically warm welcome. We are overwhelmed," said Vera Vladimirovna Pen'Kova, who is an English teacher in the Soviet Union.

The group's arrival comes after nearly a year of trying to sort through bureaucracy and arrange a visit.

The women first wrote to "Mr. Mayor" of Garden City in February. They said the Iron Curtain was lifting and they wanted to visit an American small town or rural community.

Talley, then Garden City's mayor, wrote back and said the city would love for them to visit. In their response, she became "Mrs. Talley." By the time more letters and phone calls were exchanged as arrangements progressed, she became their good friend Bonnie.

This morning, many other Garden Citians eager to become friends of the visitors crowded into the Amtrak station, sampling coffee and doughnuts and waiting for the train's arrival.

The train was scheduled to arrive at 8:05 a.m., but was running about half an hour late. The crowd chatted and passed out handmade signs printed in Cyrillic, the Russian alphabet, welcoming the visitors — although people weren't sure exactly what the signs said and one person mused it could be anything, such as "Welcome, Legionnaires."

Host families had bouquets for visitors. Flags of the Soviet Union, United States and various other countries were displayed. Balloons showed words of welcome, but a "Batman" balloon also gave a sign of American entertainment tastes.

A few people in the crowd, waiting on the train for the usual reasons and not expecting the ruckus, looked bewildered and asked what was going on.

At 8:30 a.m., Amtrak agent Jed Olcott opened the door to the tracks and announced the train was now at milepost 392.

"You are standing at milepost 402," he told the crowd, which began pouring out the door to wait on the train.

Each visitor was greeted with applause. Vice Mayor Dennis Mesa and members of the sister cities committee gave brief welcoming speeches.

"We have seen many changes during our lifetime and look forward to sharing ideas, thoughts and dreams between our two people," Mesa said.

Zina Amante, a Garden Citian who is from the Soviet Union and is a trained musician, led the Soviet group in singing a song in Russian. The crowd then sang "The Star-Spangled Banner."

The group will stay here for three months and then visit Chanute, to which the women also wrote, for another three months. They wrote to several communities in the hopes of getting a response.

Still, one mystery has been why they selected cities in Kansas. Speculating on that question before the women arrived, Talley came up with a theory.

"I think they wanted the center of the country," she said. "I think they had been told to get out of the edges and find out what it's really like."

Soboleva this morning confirmed that. First apologizing and saying her English is bad, she said the women thought that a "not large town — in the center — is more characteristic of the country."

She searched a while for the word "characteristic," but it was the one she wanted. She said the women come from Moscow, a large city, and they believe people who live in smaller towns always are more characteristic of a country.

While here, the group will experience American life and speak to organizations and service clubs. The public is invited to meet them at a covered dish dinner at 7 p.m. tomorrow at the Community Church. People should bring a covered dish and table service.

Soboleva, a physics teacher, and her son, Alexei, will stay with Gene and Donna Skinner.

See Soviets, Page 3

Talley

WAITING — A group of Garden Citians waits for the train carrying visitors from Russia.

Kansas welcomes Russians for a taste of American life

By Mike Berry
Eagle Western Kansas bureau

GARDEN CITY — The Russians have landed in Garden City, and Garden City couldn't be happier about it.

Five Russian women and three of their children arrived Friday, starting a six-month adventure of living in and learning about the United States.

Three-year-old Paul Barkley waved a Soviet flag in one fist and the Stars and Stripes in the other as he watched the welcoming ceremony at the railroad depot. Irina Dmitrievna and her teenage son, Artem, will live with Paul and his parents for the next three months.

"They're really interested in what rural American life is like," said Paul's dad, Ted Barkley. "I think they probably came to the right place."

The Soviet women and their youngsters will spend the last three months of their stay in the United States with families in Chanute.

The journey to friendship began in February, when the women picked city names at random off a U.S. map and sent blind letters to "Mr. Mayor" in several Midwestern towns. No sponsoring agency was involved; they wrote the letters because they just wanted to experience America firsthand.

Bonnie Talley, now a City Council member, was "Mr. Mayor" then, and she fielded the inquiry. Talley wasted no time starting the wheels rolling to bring Valentina Konstantinovna, her daughter, Maria, and the other women to Garden City.

"It was a crazy idea," acknowledged Vera Vladimirovna, an English teacher in the Moscow school system. The women didn't tell their husbands about their plans until they had heard from Garden City. The men were "very skeptical" about such a trip, Vladimirovna said. Now they envy the women.

"We heard so much lies about America, we wanted to see with our own eyes what America really is about. ... We never stop being surprised at the kindness of the people, their readiness to help, their readiness to smile," Vladimirovna said.

The five women flew into Washington Nov. 27, where they were greeted by U.S. Sen. Nancy Kassebaum, R-Kan. They spent part of the day strolling through shops in Alexandria, Va.

"It was a shock for me to see all that food," said Vladimirovna. "It was like 'Alice in Wonderland.'"

Food is in short supply at home. Conditions have grown worse for the masses as communism has crumbled, Vladimirovna said. "There even are bread shortages," she said. "Everybody works, but nobody gets anything but the bosses."

Love, Vera

An exchange of ideas

Russian women ready to absorb Kansas lifestyle

By Sara Peterson
The Hutchinson News

GARDEN CITY — A smile is one Kansas souvenir Valentina Zharinov will take home to the Soviet Union.

"We learn to smile here," said Mrs. Zharinov, who works as an office manager in Moscow. "I like it very much. When we go back to Russia, we will smile."

Since she arrived in Garden City in November, Mrs. Zharinov said she has been overwhelmed by the friendliness of the people. In Moscow, she said, people do not smile very much.

Her friend Tamara Sobolev agreed.

"I have never seen so many smiling faces," she said.

Mrs. Zharinov and Mrs. Sobolev are members of a unique group of Russian women living in Garden City to experience American life.

For six months, the group of five women and three of their children will study, travel and share daily life with Kansas families in Garden City, Hesston and Chanute.

Every day in America is a learning experience for the women.

"Each meeting (with Americans), I learn something," said Mrs. Sobolev, who made the trip with her 14-year-old son, Alex. "Sometimes I know about me more."

Garden City's fresh air, clean streets, spacious houses, dependable roads and well-stocked grocery stores are a sharp contrast to the life the women left in Moscow.

"Life — it is much easier here than at home," said Vera Penkov, who teaches English in a grammar school in the Soviet Union. "Here, the people relax more when they get home. They don't have as much work."

In Moscow, Mrs. Penkov said, much of their time is spent shopping for food. With the Soviet's collapsing economy, Moscow is under a blockade and the store shelves usually are empty.

Most days, the women said, they leave work with their "maybe bag" and spend hours shopping for food.

The large folding bags get their name, Mrs. Sobolev says, because

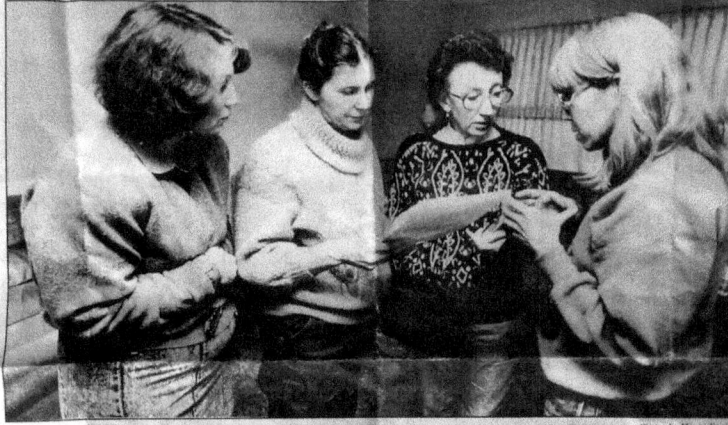

Russian citizens Tamara Sobolev, left, Vera Penkov, Valentina Zharinov, and Ira Tkatchev discuss their schedule of events during a three-month stay in Garden City.

"maybe suddenly you'll find something."

When they do find something to buy — such as fresh fruit and vegetables — they buy as much as they can carry, because no one knows when the item will be available again.

"That is why Russian women are so strong," said Mrs. Zharinov, joking about carrying the heavy bags.

On top of shopping, the women said, they don't have many of the time saving appliances — dishwashers, microwaves and clothes dryers — or the help that American women have.

"There is a different attitude toward women here," said Ira Tkatchev, who works as a computer programmer in Moscow. "Men do more housework here. I'm afraid our men aren't very good at that."

Everyday American life is what the group of friends wanted to experience when they wrote a letter last January to former Garden City Mayor Bonnie Talley.

Despite perestroika and glasnost, Soviet citizens must have an invitation from an American citizen before they can visit the United States.

None of the women knew any Americans when they decided to plan the trip.

Undaunted by this slight problem, Mrs. Zharinov came up with the idea to write letters to mayors across the United States explaining their goal and asking for an invitation.

Using an atlas, they chose cities at random and wrote blind letters.

The letter-writing campaign brought laughs from their husbands.

"Our husbands thought it was a crazy idea," Mrs. Penkov said.

The letters brought laughs in Garden City also, said Mrs. Talley, who is serving as hostess to Mrs. Zharinov and her 13-year-old daughter, Maria.

"A lot of people here didn't believe it," she said. "I thought it was fascinating."

The group drew the interest of a number of other cities around the country but the members chose Garden City because of its location.

Vladimir Lenin's picture is on the face of Soviet currency

"Kansas was in the center of America and we thought in Kansas real Americans would

See RUSSIANS, Page 12

Kansans keep Soviets busy during their stay

AT RANDOM

By DOLORES HOPE
Columnist
The Telegram

The busiest women in town for the past two months have been five women from out of town.

Five women from Russia have had few, if any, free moments since they arrived here by early morning train on Nov. 30. Ask their schedule coordinator, dispatch center keeper and booking agent Emily Barkley.

Up to the last week of January, they had made approximately 80 presentations, 55 of them in Garden City, Emily said. For many club, school and civic events and tours, all of them were on hand. At other times, however, they split up to cover a couple engagements at the same time, to show slides and answer questions.

(One woman and her son returned to Russia two weeks ago and another woman will go home Feb. 27.)

Interest in meeting and hearing the visitors spread beyond Garden City. They have been invited to 15 area towns — including Moscow, Syracuse, Cimarron, Pierceville, Hugoton, Lakin, Leoti, Liberal, Ashland, Meade, Sublette and Copeland.

In Hugoton alone, Emily said, they met and talked to around 280 people. They spent weekends in some towns.

"They have had something scheduled every single day since they arrived," said Emily. "December was moderately busy and January was exhausting. Often, they had three engagements a day. We hope to slow the pace in February down to just one appearance a day for each."

By now, Emily said, she has learned a lot about scheduling events and saying "no" when necessary. Also, the women are more comfortable about making solo appearances and voicing their preferences on where to go and what to do.

They have been to the Southwest Kansas Research Extension Center (experiment station), Reeves' Fish Farm, the rural schools and many of the city schools; they've toured system; some have participated in the Great Books program, English classes at the Adult Learning Center and thrice weekly swimming at the YMCA; and others have attended bridge parties, luncheons, a baby shower and Lamaze sessions.

Attending church services regularly with their host families has been a favorite experience for the women, Emily said.

"What they haven't had is much time to relax and to visit and compare notes with one another, shop and go about on their own."

For one week in February, they will be in Hesston and, at the end of the month, the remaining three women and two teen-agers will go to Chanute for three months.

The stay there will be different, Emily said. Instead of having one host throughout, each will be with a different family every week and there will be more trips to larger cities. In addition, Chanute officials will arrange a weekend getaway for the Russian visitors to allow them to spend time alone with one another.

Whatever else, the visitors from Moscow have not been bored so far. They may, however, have been surprised at the interest shown in them and their country.

"They've been working hard and giving a lot of themselves here," their calendar coordinator will

Love, Vera

Public Pulse

Russian visitor says thank you

As my visit draws to a close, I would like to take this opportunity to thank Garden City and southwestern Kansas residents for their warm reception. I have had a wonderful time. It has been an experience that I will never forget. I assure you that prior to my departure from Moscow, I did not envision such a reception, and I want to take this opportunity to thank all of you for being such wonderful hosts.

In particular, I would like to thank the Sister City Committee and especially Bonnie Talley, who responded to our "Mr. Mayor" letter. The enthusiastic work of Talley and the committee helped make my trip a reality. My host family, Barbara and Milton McMinimy, helped me enjoy every single moment of staying with them. It is hard for me to find proper words to express my gratefulness to them. They've become more than friends; they've become family for me.

I would also like to extend my thanks to members of the medical community. I have received care and services from them that would hardly be available to me in my country.

Also, I would like to thank the Finney County Historical Museum and staff and Bank IV for providing space and special attention to the exhibiting of my husband's paintings.

And, finally, a special thank you to the Community Church of Garden City which has generously shared its facilities to my group from Moscow.

Again, thank you all. If any of you plan to travel to Moscow, be sure to let me know, for you will always be welcome. Until we meet again, may God be with you.

VERA PENKOVA
Moscow, USSR

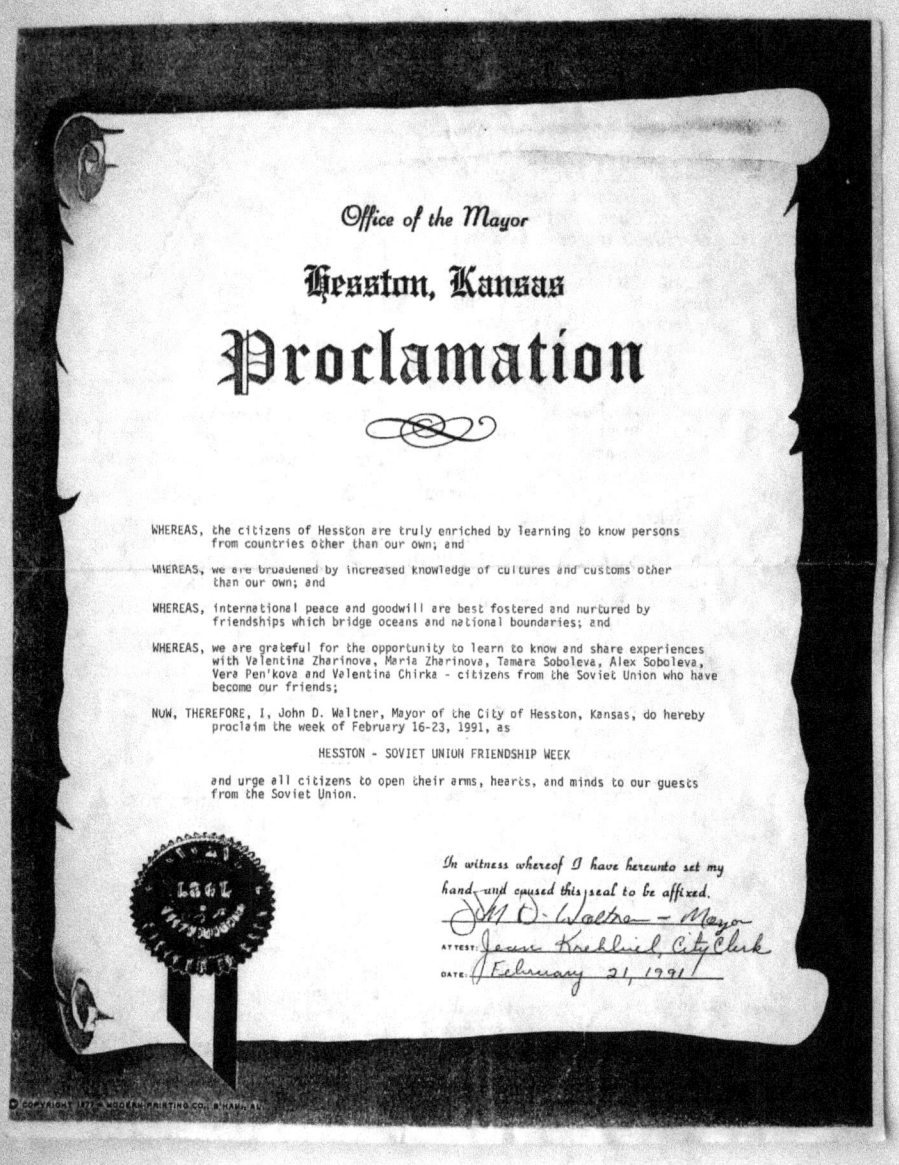

Love, Vera

Pre-coup letter arrives from a Russian visitor

AT RANDOM

By DOLORES HOPE
Columnist, The Telegram

Just a few days before the coup in the Kremlin, one of last winter's "Russian visitors" wrote to her special friends in Garden City. The four-page letter arrived last week.

The letter was cheerful and upbeat, filled with the optimism of new life. In this case, the new life has nothing to do with political changes. It revolves around her first child, a son, Andre (Andy), born a few months after she returned to Moscow.

"All my days are the same, filled with doing things for Andy and that's a lot of work (pleasure, too)," she wrote. "Fortunately we had very warm and dry summer and even now in August it is not bad. During last months, I was out with Andy all day long, coming home for feedings, so I feel like I lived outside in the forest. I knitted, read newspapers and a book and even ate there. Andy is so used to our walks that it will be difficult for him to stay at home when the weather gets worse. The other day it was rainy, but Andy wouldn't sleep at home, so I walked with him in the rain under umbrella."

To give an idea of prices in Moscow, the Russian woman quoted farmer's market prices to show how much $100 would buy. She wrote:

"For one dollar, you can buy one kilo (more than two pounds) of meat or one-half kilo of fruit or berries or 2 kilos of cottage cheese or 10 liters (a liter is roughly a quart) of milk. Prices in the shops are even lower."

The Russian woman is a teacher of English in Moscow schools and her husband is an artist. "It's a pity," she said, "that teachers get in dollars, 15 to 20 monthly ... so 100 dollars are enough to live on for two to three months.

"For poor Americans, I would recommend to come and live in Russia. They can live comfortably for 30 to 50 dollars a month (if they don't need clothes or shoes, of course — they wouldn't find such things here).

Back to Andy, she went on, "Thank God I can make some things, so we don't have to spend time and money to buy clothes for Andy. I have already made two bonnets and a sweatshirt for him. For autumn I need warm pants for him and I made them out of my old sweatshirt (sleeves for legs). Mothers with babies share ideas and we have lots of fun inventing and making things for them. My idea of using sleeves for pants is very popular. I am awfully proud."

Well-educated and with strong opinions about the political past of her native land, this Russian woman was outspoken about her feelings, all negative, for Gorbachev and Communism when she was in Garden City. Motherhood has not entirely diverted her.

She wrote, "I don't watch TV at all and sometimes hear the radio so I don't follow political events closely."

But she continued, "Yeltsin made a law that forbids party activity in enterprises and institutions but communists resist. They try to assure us that we won't survive without them. But thanks to them, we already learned to live without decent food and clothes and many other things so I think we'll be all right without party bosses too.

"The governments have changed but it is a strange change: from Communist to Democrats but somehow it happened that all Democrats are former Communists and they talk nicely but have same ways as before."

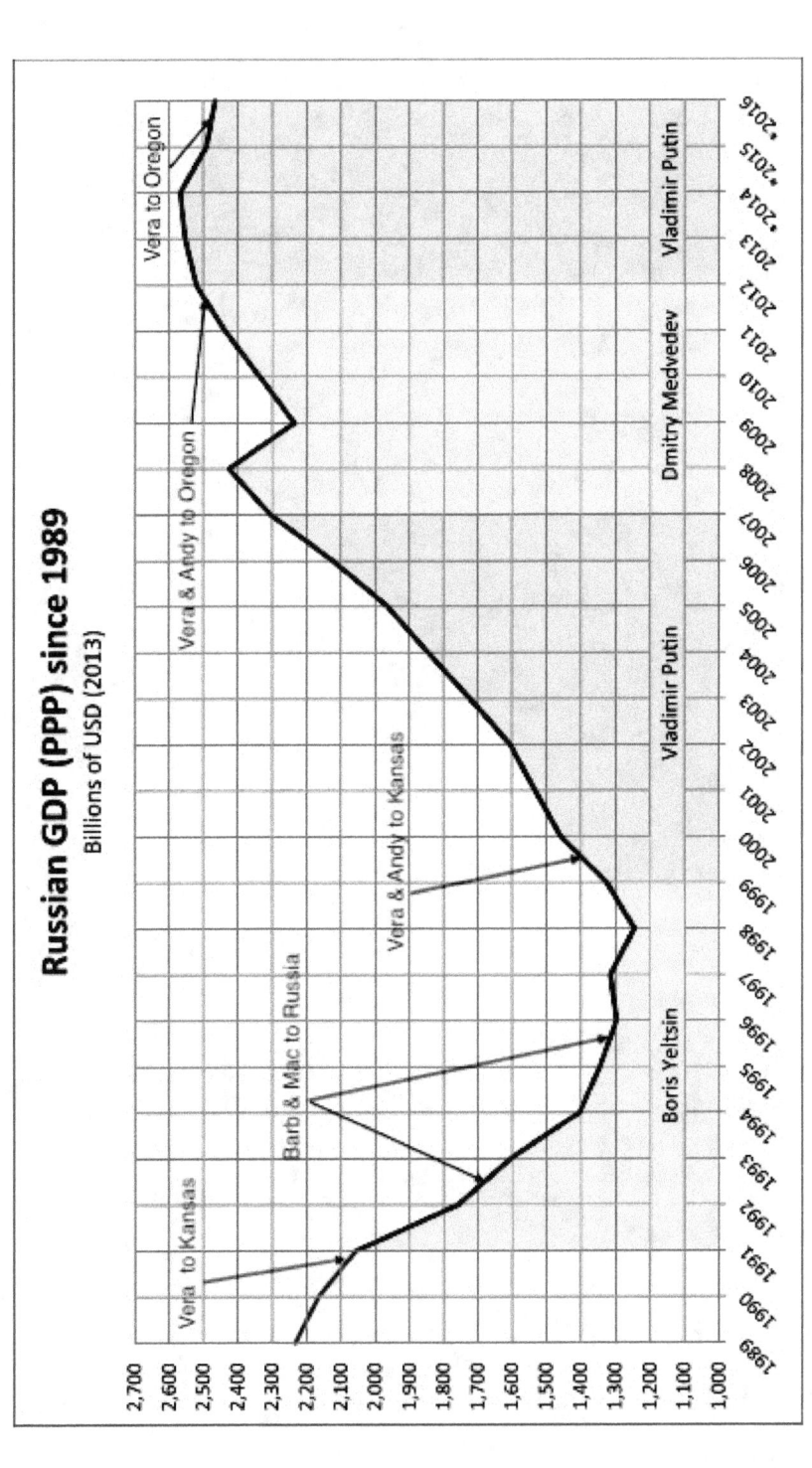

www.ingramcontent.com/pod-product-compliance
Lightning Source LLC
Chambersburg PA
CBHW052148110526
44591CB00012B/1901